Praise for *Get Up* to Speed with Online *Marketing*

D0363385

'Not to be part of the social media revolution is to miss out. Jon Reed really gets it and shows you how to join in.'

SUZANNE MOORE, COLUMNIST, *THE GUARDIAN*

'In a fast-paced digital world where it seems like everyone is playing catch up, Get Up to Speed with Online Marketing *is packed with the practical, no-nonsense insight that allows anyone marketing their business not only to keep up but to get ahead.'*

JUSTIN COOKE, CEO, POSSIBLE AND CHAIR,
BRITISH INTERACTIVE MEDIA ASSOCIATION

'Why waste money and resources trying to tweak your marketing strategy for the online age? Jon Reed has done it for you by giving you the tools to join the social marketing revolution taking place. This practical and invaluable book should be on the desk of anyone wanting to make a success of their online presence.'

CLAUDIO CONCHA, HEAD OF DIGITAL MEDIA, BIG LOTTERY FUND

'Facebook, LinkedIn, Twitter or YouTube? If you want to figure out how to effectively use social media to build your business, Jon Reed's straightforward and practical guide will help you figure out which one to use and where to start.'

SUZANNE KAVANAGH, DIRECTOR OF MARKETING AND
MEMBERSHIP SERVICES, ASSOCIATION OF LEARNED
AND PROFESSIONAL SOCIETY PUBLISHERS

Get Up to Speed with Online Marketing

**The Twitter account for this book is:
@getuptospeed**

Get Up to Speed with Online Marketing

How to use websites, blogs, social networking and more to promote your business

2nd Edition

Jon Reed

PEARSON

Harlow, England • London • New York • Boston • San Francisco • Toronto • Sydney • Auckland • Singapore • Hong Kong
Tokyo • Seoul • Taipei • New Delhi • Cape Town • São Paulo • Mexico City • Madrid • Amsterdam • Munich • Paris • Milan

PEARSON EDUCATION LIMITED
Edinburgh Gate
Harlow CM20 2JE
United Kingdom
Tel: +44 (0)1279 623623
Web: www.pearson.com/uk

First published 2011 (print)
Second edition published 2013 (print and electronic)

Pearson Education is not responsible for the content of third-party internet sites.

ISBN: 978-1-292-00116-6 (print)
        978-1-292-00117-3 (PDF)
        978-1-292-00118-0 (ePub)

British Library Cataloguing-in-Publication Data
A catalogue record for the print edition is available from the British Library

Library of Congress Cataloging-in-Publication Data
Reed, Jon, 1971-
   Get up to speed with online marketing : how to use websites, blogs, social networking
   and more to promote your business / Jon Reed. – 2nd edition.
     pages cm
   Includes index.
   ISBN 978-1-292-00116-6
   1. Internet marketing. 2. Social media. 3. Small business–Management. I. Title.
   HF5415. 1265.R43 2013
   658.8'72--dc23
                              2013028573

10 9 8 7 6 5 4 3 2 1
17 16 15 14 13

Cover design by Dan Mogford, background image © Alexandra Khrobostova/Shutterstock.com

Print edition typeset in 9/13pt Helvetica LT Pro by 30
Print edition printed in Great Britain by Henry Ling Ltd, at the Dorset Press, Dorchester,
Dorset

NOTE THAT ANY PAGE CROSS REFERENCES REFER TO THE PRINT EDITION

Contents

Part Four Get out there

Part Five Get help

Acknowledgements

I would like to thank the business owners whose online marketing success stories appear in this edition, plus Eloise Cook, Lucy Carter, Emma Devlin, Rhian McKay, Paul East and Amy Joyner at Pearson – and Liz Gooster who commissioned the book in the first place. I am also grateful to everyone who has attended my workshops and lectures, and to readers of the first edition. Your feedback has contributed to the development of this new edition of *Get Up to Speed with Online Marketing*.

About the author

Jon Reed has been teaching social media marketing since its earliest days and has helped thousands of people use it via his books, blogs and courses. He previously worked in publishing for 10 years, including as publishing director for McGraw-Hill. Jon is probably best known for his website Publishing Talk (**www.publishingtalk.eu**), an online learning resource for authors and publishers with one of the largest Twitter followings in the publishing world (@publishingtalk).

Jon provides social media training through his company Reed Media (**www.reedmedia.eu**) and regularly runs workshops and in-house training. He has also run a series of *Guardian* Masterclasses on social media marketing and lectured on the subject at several UK universities, including Kingston University, City University and Birkbeck, University of London. Follow him on Twitter at @jonreed, or at @getuptospeed for tips and updates about this book.

Preface to the second edition

Sexual intercourse may have begun in 1963 (according to Philip Larkin) – but social media began in 2006. That's the year that Facebook became open to everyone, Twitter launched and Google bought YouTube. Four years later the first edition of this book was written. Another three years on and much has changed: Instagram, Pinterest and Google+ have come on the scene, and the web has become a more visual medium. Most importantly, social media has become a mainstream part of business and culture.

Yet the principles and approach to using social media to market your business remain the same: start with your objectives, choose appropriate tools and measure your results. The tools evolve, new ones come along, others fall out of fashion and sometimes disappear. It can be hard to keep up – but you don't need to follow every social media fad and fashion. You do need to be up to speed with the basics, and have a clear marketing strategy.

This edition has new and updated case studies throughout, new material on Instagram, new chapters on Pinterest and Google +, and thorough updates on the other tools. It also has a stronger focus on your marketing strategy – advice on what works, why it works, and best practice for using it effectively for your business – rather than the basics of, say, how to set up a Twitter account. If you *do* need help with the basics, you can now find some illustrated step-by-step tutorials on the website instead at **www.getuptospeed.biz**.

Some chapters have also been dropped from this edition. While virtual worlds were attracting much attention some years back, for most of us today they aren't going to be a significant part of our online marketing mix. And although social bookmarking sites such as Delicious, Digg and StumbleUpon are still important, I don't really think you need to spend much time on these sites as a small business owner. It is far more important simply to make it easy for other people to bookmark your content – and that is covered in the blogging chapter. It is a wiser investment to spend your time on what is now the internet's most important social bookmarking site – Pinterest – and to get to grips with the basics of Google+, which is growing in importance. If you do still want to read the chapters on virtual worlds and social bookmarking, you can now also find these on the website.

This edition focuses on those online marketing and social media tools most likely to provide tangible results for most businesses. I know your time is precious – and there is a limit to how many tools you need to use, or even be aware of. You don't need all of them, and this book will help you decide where to focus your efforts. You also don't need to spend ages reading up on the ever-growing field of social media. You just need a primer in the basics of online marketing, an overview of the tools available, and some practical ideas to get you started right away. What you need is to get up to speed!

About this book

If you are a new or aspiring business owner, the challenges and tasks you face can appear daunting. How do you find time to market your product or service as well as doing the work required to deliver it? This book will show you some quick wins and show you easy and effective ways to reach out to your market today. If you work for a larger business, you will also find plenty of tips here to inform and inspire you.

This book will help you get up to speed with the basics of social media marketing, as well as websites, email marketing and search engine marketing (SEM); and it will also give you a solid foundation for your online marketing strategy. You will gain an understanding of how to align your online marketing with business objectives, and practical tips for how to manage the workload and measure your results. An extensive glossary cuts through the jargon; and if you're not quite ready to take the plunge yourself, or really don't have the time, there is also advice on how to find someone to help you with it.

We will look at case studies of businesses that have succeeded with online marketing tools, in the '... in action' section of most chapters. The case studies and other businesses mentioned along the way in this book may surprise you: most are not technology businesses, as you might imagine. They include hotels, electricians, property developers, an import/export agent, a carpentry blogger, and companies that sell jeans, jewellery, beer, cheesecake, wedding stationery and shoes – people just like you. There are fewer opportunities to be a 'first mover' in social media these days – but if you think that no one in your industry bothers with it, congratulations! You are in the rare and privileged position of having a competitive advantage in your industry. This can also apply if you are not the first, but your competition just isn't doing it that well.

The new marketing isn't austerity marketing but it does also have advantages when funds are tight. If your business is struggling as a result of the global recession, it can be tempting to cut back on your marketing. Actually, it is the very worst time to do so. Less marketing never leads to more sales. However, by following the principles in this book, you needn't spend a fortune. You may even be able to cut back your marketing budget while increasing your reach.

The companion website

Online marketing is a constantly evolving field, with new social media tools cropping up all the time. It can be hard to keep up. For updates on the information in this book, take a look at the accompanying website at **www.getuptospeed.biz**, which includes:

→ illustrated step-by-step tutorials to help you get started with the tools quickly;

→ a blog with further advice on each of the online marketing tools covered in this book;

→ additional case studies from business owners;

→ a free marketing plan template and five-day email course on planning your online marketing.

You can also get in touch with me via the site, and submit a case study sharing your own experience of online marketing.

Get up to speed faster!

If you're really pushed for time, can't wait to get started with all those social media tools, or just need a bit more help getting started, there is now an online course that accompanies this book. This is based on a face-to-face course I have run for small businesses for several years. For the first time, this is now available to anyone, anywhere, from the comfort of your own home and at your own pace. Find out more at **www.getuptospeed.biz/course**.

Get in touch

Social media is a two-way conversation, and I want to hear from you! Connect with me online, let me know what you did or didn't like, what you would like to see in the next edition, and tell me about your experience of online marketing. You can also follow me on Twitter at @getuptospeed or @jonreed, find links to me on all the other social sites I use at **www.getuptospeed.biz**, or email me at **jon@getuptospeed.biz**.

For now, I wish you the best of luck with your business. Whether you're aspiring, brand new or more established, I hope you will find this book a useful guide for focusing your marketing efforts where they are most effective.

Introduction

Social media is mainstream. Are you up to speed?

If you've bought this book you may need little convincing that social media marketing is something you need to do. In 2010 you might have needed some persuading. Today, there is no longer a battle between social media and mainstream marketing. Social media *is* the mainstream. Facebook has over a billion users, Twitter has over 600 million accounts, and people spend more time on social networks than they do on email.

Concentrate on being *findable*.

While 'everyone else is doing it' isn't a good enough reason in itself, if your competitors are on Twitter and Facebook and you're not, you may be missing out. More importantly, it is likely that the very people you are trying to reach with your marketing messages are also on these sites. If your customers use social media, you need to use it too. The user numbers speak for themselves: these sites are neither faddy nor niche. A broad range of people use these sites, and some are your ideal clients, customers and prospects. Concentrate on being *findable*. If you can make your products or services easy to find online, you're halfway there.

Social media is mainstream. If you're not using it yet, you need to get up to speed – and quick. The good news is that you don't need to do everything, and it's easy to learn the basics. This book will show you which bits to focus on and why.

I'm a publisher – so are you

My background is in publishing. I worked for various publishing companies for 10 years before starting my own business. In 2005 I studied part-time for a Postgraduate Diploma in Digital Media Management at Birkbeck, University of London – one of the courses

I now teach on. This was the first time I came across social media – or 'Web 2.0' as everyone was calling it then. I started out building websites, creating digital media – and advising on social media. I narrowed my specialism to social media and continued to share what I had learned with others. Teaching is central to everything I do, whether it's lecturing, running a workshop or in-house training, writing books or producing online learning materials.

Yet I've almost come full circle, because part of my business is now publishing magazines, books and other learning resources at Publishing Talk (**www.publishingtalk.eu**) – the online community of authors and publishers I have built up over the last few years. So, you might still call me a publisher. But here's the thing: whatever your business is, if you are using social media *you too are a publisher*. My experience of publishing, social media and running a small business has made me realise just how interconnected these things are.

You don't have to run a content business or a training business to benefit from social media. You don't need to run a high-tech business or sell 'information products'. You don't even need to sell products from a website. You just need to have a presence online, use the social networks that your customers and prospects use, and give them a reason to connect with you. But you can't just do a few tweets: you need to publish some content. That content is the starting point for your online marketing campaign, as you use it to reach and engage with potential customers and clients who will seek it out with their online searches.

The principles apply whether you are a carpenter or a bike shop. Anyone with an internet connection and a bit of creativity can now communicate with the world via the written word, audio, video and images. You don't even need a computer – you can do it from your smartphone. A radical power shift of content creation and distribution from large media institutions to individuals has taken place over the past few years: everyone is a publisher now.

The evolving web

When did we all join the media business? How did the internet make this possible? When British computer scientist Tim Berners-Lee invented this thing called the World Wide Web in 1990, he could scarcely have imagined what it has become today: a ubiquitous part of our everyday lives. Fully integrated into our social lives, an essential business tool, and a creative multimedia platform. It has also progressively become a more media-rich visual medium, and it is now with us wherever we go thanks to that other technological trend of the age: mobile phones. These trends are interconnected, and now have a direct impact on the way we do business.

The social web

What is sometimes referred to as the 'social web' is now really just the web. We no longer say 'motor car' – we just say 'car'. It is taken as read that our cars are motorised. So it is has become with the internet – it is a given that we use the internet to connect with our friends, express our personalities and opinions, publish our photos or watch a video. It is the same with online marketing. Social media has just become the way we do that.

Social media is the currency of the social web. Most people might think of it as a collection of tools, websites and online services. For our purposes it is also helpful to think of it as an approach to marketing, and a subset of online marketing tools, which more broadly include websites, search engine marketing and email marketing. If you need convincing of just how much of the web is social, you need only look up the top sites ranked by Alexa (**www.alexa.com/topsites**). The top three have for a long time been Google, Facebook and YouTube; with Wikipedia, Twitter, Blogger, LinkedIn, Pinterest and WordPress.com all occupying high positions.

Having a presence on social sites is a necessary but not sufficient prerequisite for successful social media marketing. Yes, you might have a gazillion followers – but are they buying anything? It's easy to get carried away with the metrics and forget why you're on social networks in the first place – to engage with your community. This book will help you with that.

What does this mean for you?

→ Ensure you have a presence on the main social websites, so that you are findable in the places your customers spend their online time.

→ If you want to build relationships with your customers, social media is now the way to do it online.

The visual web

Have you noticed how visual a medium the web has become recently? In some ways this is a continuation of a long-term trend. I remember when the internet was all text, with the occasional picture that took forever to download. Since then, it has steadily become more visual. The web then and now is like comparing an academic monograph to a highly illustrated coffee table book. Which would you rather read?

There are two reasons for this: improvements in technology, and diminishing attention spans. Super-fast wireless broadband means pictures download instantly and video streams effortlessly for many people. Technological developments have made photo sharing and video sharing sites possible – and popular. The other reason is our shrinking attention spans which, online, are *tiny*. This is understandable – there is just so much online information to wade through these days, who has time to read lengthy paragraphs of text? We want succinct blog posts, short videos, and *pictures*. Something that will show us at a glance if we've found what we're looking for. Something that will attract our attention and draw us in. Something that looks nice that we want to click on and share.

This is one reason why Pinterest is such a success. As an online scrapbook of images it is attractive – even addictive. As a social bookmarking site, it drives far more traffic to websites than previous text-based ones such as Delicious. There's a reason why Facebook paid so much to acquire Instagram. But it is not just new, visual social networks springing up: the old ones are getting more visual too. Facebook's timeline layout gives more weight to images. Facebook, Twitter and Google+ all have prominent header images on profiles now. This is becoming the norm for what social networks look like.

What does this mean for you?

→ Make sure you use plenty of images on your social networking sites.

→ Make sure you use images on *any* web page or blog post that you want people to 'pin' to Pinterest – they can't share your content if you don't have a pinnable image!

The mobile web

One of the things that has enabled the rapid growth of social media is the increased uptake of smartphones and mobile web browsing. More and more of us access the internet on the move from our phones. The International Telecommunications Union has even predicted that mobile access to the internet will soon overtake access from desktop computers. In some parts of the world, such as Africa, mobile phones have been the primary access point to the internet for a while already.

It is not just mobile access to the internet itself: it's all those *apps*. All your favourite social media sites and services are available as iPhone or Android smartphone apps. Some, such as Instagram, are *only* available if you have a smartphone. The fact that many of us update our Twitter or Facebook status on the move – often including photos and/or location information – is what has driven the growth of these networks. We are entering a world where all media is social, and all our social interactions are mediated via apps and updates.

What does this mean for you?

→ Make sure your websites are accessible from mobile devices – discuss this with your web designer, or choose a WordPress theme that states it displays well on smartphones.

→ Take advantage of all those social networking apps by using them on your smartphone – it will save you time, and enable you to react quickly on the move.

The marketing revolution

The evolution of the web has in turn led to a marketing revolution. The change is not just in technology but in culture. Hard selling has been replaced by social engagement. Instead of indiscriminately shouting sterile corporate marketing messages at people who may or may not be interested in your product or service, today you can find people who are *already interested* in what you have to offer, by tapping into pre-existing online communities of interest – or even by creating your own. In today's competitive marketplace you need to be findable. You need to go where your customers are, and engage them in conversation.

You need to go where your customers are.

This is a shift from 'push' marketing to 'pull' marketing, where we are attracting people towards us with engaging, interesting, valuable content that they will seek out. If you can tap into those communities of interest, you won't ever need to sell again – people will come looking for you.

You might think of social marketing as permission-based marketing, word-of-mouth marketing, or conversational marketing. One phrase I came across a little while ago is *martini marketing* – in the sense of the 1970s Martini TV ad that used the strapline: 'any time, any place, anywhere'. That really sums up how marketing should work these days – going where your market is, reaching them with content they want, when and where they want you to. The rise of the mobile web means this is now often on the move. This is a shift away from *megaphone marketing* – randomly shouting your message at a heterogeneous mass of people. By using social media, you are making yourself visible to niche communities of interest. You can engage them with useful content, and build a relationship with them.

Social media marketing works for small businesses because it focuses on building customer relationships rather than sterile marketing campaigns. Resist the temptation to use that safe, impersonal corporate voice – stick your head above the parapet and be yourself!

And there is an advantage to being small. Because social media is a personal medium where authenticity matters, it is not always easy for big corporations to use. It's perfect if you are a small business or entrepreneur: you can build trust and make connections by using your personality and being genuine. The social media marketing revolution has arrived, and you can be part of it.

Get strategic

Part One

Online marketing 101

Chapter One

Online marketing 101

Before we jump in with all the exciting tools available, let's take a step back and think about what you want to achieve. Just because it is quick, easy and free to set up an account with WordPress, Facebook, Twitter, Pinterest or YouTube doesn't mean you should. Like any form of marketing, your starting point should be your marketing aims and objectives, then identifying your community and where they hang out – *then* you choose appropriate tools to reach them. This chapter will give you a crash course in online marketing strategy, and help you understand some key principles of social media that will enable you to use any tool appropriately and effectively.

What is online marketing?

Online marketing does a lot of the same things that traditional marketing does – it just does them more cheaply and effectively with greater reach.

There are almost two billion people online. Some of them are your ideal clients or customers. If you can reach even a tiny fraction of them, you will have a viable business. The internet has brought enormous benefits to the way we market our businesses. A website is like a virtual shopfront that is always open. Email reaches targeted audiences with news of our latest products. A blog provides regular information for customers and prospects, which they can comment on. Social networks enable us to make direct connections with people who are interested in our wares. However specialised our niche, there is a global market for it online, which not only can we reach but, by increasing our visibility online, will also come looking for us.

A website is like a virtual shopfront that is always open.

You may be familiar with the traditional marketing concept of the 'sales funnel'. It describes the stages through which potential customers pass from being a diffuse mass market of people who are

FIGURE 1.1 Online versus traditional marketing methods

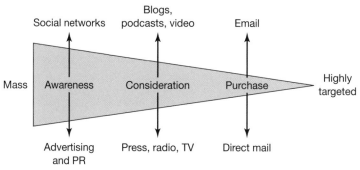

unaware of your existence to a highly targeted loyal customer who comes back for more. It also describes which marketing methods to use at which stage (Figure 1.1).

Online marketing methods loosely map on to traditional methods, but at every stage you are making yourself visible to people who will seek you out, and engaging a highly targeted audience, rather than broadcasting an indiscriminate message and hoping for the best. Word of mouth is the Holy Grail of marketing – and very difficult to achieve offline. But it is turbo-charged with online marketing.

Why online marketing works for business

Online marketing is:

→ **Affordable**. Because it is cheaper than traditional marketing, you can use it to punch above your weight.

→ **Effective**. People spend more time online – use online marketing to reach your market where they are.

→ **Authentic**. Tools such as blogging and podcasting are personal media. You can use them credibly as a small business owner, in a way that is hard for large corporates to do.

Given the amount of time people spend on the internet, particularly on social sites, it makes sense to join in. Specific reasons why online marketing works for business include:

1 **Drive traffic to your site**. Your website is the hub of your business, and the aim of your online marketing activities is to drive traffic to it. This is one reason why Pinterest is such an interesting site – it drives a *lot* of referral traffic.

2 **New ways to connect with your market**. By establishing a presence on social sites that your market uses you'll become visible to a new set of prospects.

3 **Build trust**. People always prefer to do business with people they know. Your clients and customers can get to know you through your online presence.

4 **Start a conversation**. A two-way dialogue with your customers and prospects is much more effective than a one-way broadcast of your marketing message.

5 **Create value**. Part of the secret of online marketing is creating useful content and giving it away. If you can create a useful resource or interesting content targeted at your niche, they will keep coming back for more.

6 **Build communities**. Think of your market as a 'community of interest', built around a particular topic related to your business. You can also approach this idea the other way around: it can be possible to build products around your online community.

7 **Provide quick, up-to-date information**. The 'breaking news' aspect of many forms of online marketing makes it ideal for announcements about new products or services, special offers, or simply valuable topical information about your sector or area of expertise. Twitter in particular is great for this.

8 **Data capture**. Building a database of potential customers is a core aim of your email marketing campaign. You can use social media to convert passive followers to signups to your email list.

9 **Market research**. Use social media to ask customers for feedback on your products or services, or create an online questionnaire using **www.surveymonkey.com** and market it through your online marketing channels.

Get Up to Speed with Online Marketing

10 **Low-cost, low-risk, effective**. Most of the tools are available either free or very cheap – though the investment is often in time rather than money. The risks of using social media and communicating openly with your market are low, so long as you follow the principles in this book, and are far outweighed by the benefits you will gain.

Core principles of social media

There are certain unwritten rules of using social media, and people don't like it when you break them. Understanding of the culture of social media is important. If you adhere to the following principles, you shouldn't go too far wrong, whichever tool you use:

1 **Be authentic, open, transparent**. Don't pass yourself off as something or someone you are not. Behave in a professional way, but don't be afraid to use your personal voice. The good thing about being a small business is that you don't need to get your communications approved by a committee or signed off by five people. You can just do it. Be yourself, be authentic, and people will trust you.

2 **Don't go for the hard sell**. Don't focus too much on selling products – provide useful content that your community will value. That content will 'warm up' your prospects for a later sale – particularly if you are selling something related to the content you are sharing.

3 **Build social currency**. Establishing a social media presence gives you 'permission' to use it for marketing. Once you have been on various social sites for a while, you have more credibility: people will take you more seriously and listen to what you have to say.

4 **Don't view it as just another marketing channel**. Social media is a fundamentally different approach to marketing. Using it is a commitment – not a tactic or a campaign. Don't treat it simply as something that you 'bolt on' to your existing campaign.

5 **Don't treat it as a one-way broadcast medium**. Social media becomes much more interesting, and effective, when it facilitates a

conversation between you and your community of interest. Reply to some of your tweets, retweet others – it's not all about you.

6 **Be clear about responsibilities**. If you are a micro-business or sole trader, it will probably be you maintaining all of this. But if there are several of you working on the business, it pays to be clear about who is responsible for updating what, and how often. For larger organisations you might appoint a social media manager or establish a cross-departmental committee to work out some policies and guidelines.

7 **Be patient**. Social media needs a long-term approach. A new blog takes a good six months of fairly regular updates to establish itself and build a following. You will need to spend time and effort building and maintaining your online presence before it translates into sales. But that online presence, once established, will continue to build and provide you with an essential source of potential clients and customers.

There are so many tools. Where do you begin?

It's true, there are a lot of online marketing tools out there now that enable you to build relationships with your prospects and customers. And most of them are free. Where on earth do you start?

First of all, you don't have to use everything. You can pick and choose. Not every tool is right for every business, and they need to be understood in the wider context of online marketing. Many of your activities on social networks will be aimed at driving traffic to your website, or encouraging people to sign up to your email newsletter. These things work best together.

New tools crop up all the time too, making social media seem harder than ever to stay abreast of. Instagram, Pinterest and Google+ are the big ones since the last edition of this book. What will come next? It is more important to focus on your approach than the tools. If you have a sound marketing strategy, you can apply this to new tools that come along. And, while there are plenty of pundits who will speculate about the Next Big Thing in social media, where the internet is headed, or the future of marketing, as a business owner you don't need to worry about any of that. You don't need to be ahead of the curve – in fact it's better if you're not. The Shiny New Thing might not be here for long, and there might not be enough of your customers using it – yet. Focus instead on being bang on trend: using proven online tools and social networks to reach them where they are. You can afford to take a 'wait and see' attitude to new tools as they crop up. Start with the established tools, keep an eye on the new ones, and see which take off. Does a new tool look like an interesting new way to connect with your community? Are your customers using it yet? If not, don't worry about it.

You don't need to be a tech head to use social media. You don't need to know the detail of every function of every tool you use – and this book will help you stay focused on the most important bits. The important thing is your business, your passions and your ideas. It is more important to have a message, some compelling content and a bit of creativity. The rest you can learn as you go along. The content that you reach people with is more important than the tools you use to reach them. Tapping into communities of interest is a key goal of social media marketing. And communities are built around content, not technology.

You don't need to be a tech head to use social media.

What will really help you stay focused is an online marketing plan. We'll take a look at how to do that in the next chapter.

Your online marketing plan

Chapter Two

Your online marketing plan

You know that management-speak mantra 'fail to plan and plan to fail'? Well, there is some truth in it. If you don't spend a bit of time planning your online marketing, you may not fail, but you will probably waste valuable time that you could have spent doing something more useful. You risk investing time and resources in, say, creating a bespoke Facebook page, only to discover that Facebook isn't really a useful tool for your business.

The other common pitfall with online marketing planning is starting with the tools rather than the people you are trying to reach with them. Social media tools are not, in themselves, the connection with your customers: they are simply tools that you use to connect with customers. As Jeremiah Owyang of web-strategist.com says: 'Stop fondling the hammers and nails. Instead, focus on what's really important, the guests you want to attract and what type of house they want.'

Your one-page marketing plan

If you do some marketing planning first, you can save wasted time and effort, and avoid alienating your community by using the tools inappropriately. Yes, if you're writing a college assignment or seeking investment you probably will need a reasonably lengthy document; but if, like most of us, you don't have the luxury of time, you can write your marketing plan in a single page. What's more, you *should* be able to distill your entire marketing plan into one page. It's a good discipline that will keep you focused on the core aims of your business.

Here is your one-page fill-in-the-blanks marketing plan. You can also download this as a PDF template from the website, and get some further tips on planning your marketing by email, at **www.getuptospeed.biz/ plan-your-online-marketing**.

The purpose of the marketing programme for _____ is to:

Our target market is:

Our community can be found at:

We plan to use the following social media marketing tools:

Tool *Pick at least one content tool (e.g. blog) and at least one outreach tool (e.g. Twitter)*	Call to action *E.g. sign up to newsletter; visit website*	Measurement *E.g. number of subscribers, group members, Twitter followers*
1.		
2.		
3.		
4.		
5.		

Five questions to ask yourself before you start

Your approach, and the questions you ask yourself, should be just the same as for any of your marketing efforts:

1 **What are my marketing aims and objectives?** Like any form of marketing, this is the starting point – not the marketing tool itself.

2 **Who is my target market?** Know your audience. What is your niche? What unique value can you offer?

3 **Where can I find them?** Where does your market hang out? Use online tools to find your community of interest and tap into it.

4 **Which tools are most appropriate to use?** Which tools will both reach your market and be possible for you to manage realistically?

5 **How will I measure my results?** How will you know if you are successful? What metrics will you use?

Note that the choice of tools comes way down the list. It pays to think strategically about how you choose and use the tools described in this book – which the following chapters will help you do. For now, you can work your way through this chapter (or the five-day email course) to fill in the blanks on the marketing plan template. Or you may wish to read more of this book first, and come back to it later.

Think strategically about how you choose and use the tools.

Define your goals

Step one is to decide what it is that you are trying to do. You are not trying to 'start a blog'. You are trying to promote yourself to an identifiable niche market – and one of the ways in which you might do that is (for example) with a blog. It is very tempting to start with the tools themselves – but you should always make your marketing aims and objectives your starting point.

What is it that you are marketing? Examples include: your business, a charity, a conference, a band, a specific product or service, a book – or just yourself. Think about how broadly or narrowly focused your marketing campaign will be – will it be a single product or your entire organisation?

What are your marketing aims?

What is the purpose of your marketing programme? Think carefully about what you want to achieve, so that you will know when you've been successful. Examples include:

→ raising awareness of a new brand;

→ differentiating your product from its competitors;

- → increasing sales;
- → communicating the benefits of a new product or service;
- → building an email list.

Fill in the first line of your online marketing plan template with what it is that you are marketing, and your primary marketing aim.

What are your marketing objectives?

You might also wish to set yourself specific marketing objectives. Marketing objectives are different to marketing aims. They are more specific and highly measurable. You may have come across setting 'SMART' objectives before, such as when conducting appraisals or managing a project. It's an acronym that stands for:

- → **Specific**. Is your objective a specific enough goal? If it is more general, it might be an aim rather than an objective.
- → **Measurable**. Is it measurable? We will look more at measurement later in this chapter.
- → **Achievable**. How realistic is your objective? Can you benchmark it against the competition, or against other marketing campaigns you have completed and evaluated in the past?
- → **Relevant**. Is your marketing objective central to your business? Will it help you achieve a specific business priority?
- → **Time-specific**. By when will your objective be complete? Within two months? By the end of the financial year? Put a specific date on it.

A marketing aim might be 'to increase sales'. An example of a SMART marketing objective would be 'to sell 20 workshop places within the next two months'. You can use the one-page online marketing plan at the level of an overall marketing aim, or to plan your marketing for a specific objective.

Find your community

The next step is to think about who you are trying to market your product or service to, and where you might reach them.

Who is your community of interest?

Online marketing works best in niches. Consider your positioning against the competition. Questions to ask yourself include:

- → What do you offer that is unique?
- → Who, exactly, is your product or service aimed at?
- → What would your ideal customer look like?

You are ideally trying to reach an identifiable niche community online. A community that gathers around a particular topic or interest. A *community of interest*.

How will you reach them?

Once you have your own blog, website or podcast you might be able to create a community that you can subsequently sell products or services to. That can be a good approach, though it is rather a long-term one. There is likely to be a pre-existing online community of interest that you can reach by choosing the right tools.

Ten ways to find your community

So where do you find them? Where does your community of interest hang out online? You can find out a lot by doing some searches. Search isn't just about Google these days – people also search for the information they're interested in on Twitter, Facebook, LinkedIn, YouTube, etc. – and this should be your starting point too. Here are 10 things you can do to find your community of interest online and tap into it (don't feel you have to do them all!)

1 Do a Google search to find blogs in your area of interest (you can filter search results to show only blogs).

2 Use Google Alerts (**www.google.com/alerts**) to keep abreast of keywords you want to track online. Google Alerts are email updates of the latest relevant Google search results in your topic area, and help you monitor the web for new content. Use Social Mention (**www.socialmention.com**) to set up social media alerts – like Google Alerts but for social media.

3 Search for keywords relating to your product or service on social networks. Are there LinkedIn Groups, Google+ Communities or Facebook Groups built around a topic that is relevant to your business? Are there topic-based Twitter accounts dedicated to it? Use the Twitter directory WeFollow to find the top accounts in your area. Is there a proliferation of pinners pinning images relevant to your product on Pinterest? Keyword searches will give you an idea of the interest in your niche on various networks.

4 Search LinkedIn Groups for discussions about your industry. Could LinkedIn be a place for you to contribute to discussions and showcase your expertise?

5 Search Google+ Communities for topic-based forums you could contribute to.

6 Go through the process of setting up a Facebook ad, selecting the demographic and profile keywords you want to target – but stop before you buy your ad! As you narrow down your criteria, Facebook will give you a number: the number of people on Facebook who you could reach with your ad. This will give you an idea of your market size on Facebook, and help you decide if this is a worthwhile place for you to be.

7 Is there a visual element to your business? Search Flickr for relevant groups that you can contribute images or discussions to. Search Instagram for topic hashtags that you might use to run a contest to engage users. Search Pinterest for pins and boards in your topic area. Is this a place where people might want to share images from (and links to) your website?

8 Search iTunes for podcasts in your area. Are there any? Is this a place people are likely to seek out information relating to your business? Is there a gap you can fill with your niche?

9 Search YouTube for videos in your topic area. Look at the number of views. If there are videos on YouTube receiving a lot of views, this might indicate a ready and willing video audience that you can reach with your own videos.

10 If you want to take social media monitoring to a new level, use a service such as radian6 or uberVU to discover what people are saying about your brand, industry or competitors online.

The tools that you use to monitor keywords and conversations online are often referred to as *listening tools*. For a very large brand, this might be the most important part of their social media strategy. For a small business, it might just mean doing a few searches.

Choose your marketing tools

You now know what your marketing goals are. You've thought about your target market, positioning and niche. You've done a bit of research into where your community of interest hangs out online. Now it's time to think about how to reach them.

There are so many online marketing tools, it can be hard to know where to start. I find it helpful to think of your options as a series of concentric circles (Figure 2.1).

At the centre of things is your product or service – the thing you want to sell. Wrapped around that is your business website – the hub of your online marketing. The ultimate aim of most of your marketing effort is to drive people here.

Another key aim is to build an email marketing list. Your email newsletter will provide specific calls to action leading people to buy from you – and most often will also drive people to your site. And the main call to action on your website will be to sign up to your newsletter.

Your next layer is social media. Your social media efforts will be geared to driving people to your website: it's all about driving people towards the centre of that circle. But which will you use? I find it helps simplify things if you categorise them into *content tools* and *outreach tools*.

FIGURE 2.1 Choosing online marketing tools

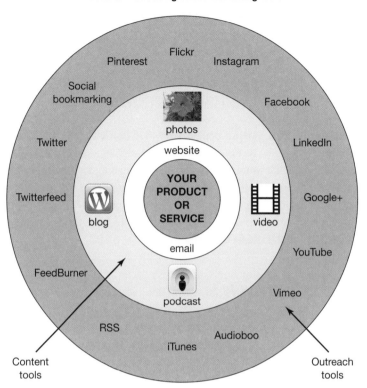

→ **Content tools** comprise the four main content types found on the internet: text, images, audio and video. These translate to the social media content you will create: blogs, photos, podcasts and online video. This is your starting point, and your first layer of social media. It is important to provide useful, informative, valuable content that is findable and 'pass-on-able' by the communities of interest you want to reach. Content tools are covered in Part 3.

→ **Outreach tools** are, essentially, everything else – but particularly social networks. This is your outer layer of social media. You will use these tools to disseminate and raise awareness of the social media content you create, as well as engaging your community in conversation. They include Facebook, LinkedIn, Twitter, Pinterest and Google+. Outreach tools are covered in Part 4.

When you're planning your social media marketing campaign, you should choose at least one content tool and at least one outreach tool. Which ones should you select? The research you did to find your community will help you decide. Going where your market is is important. But it is also important to be realistic, and choose tools that work for you. Not everyone has the time to maintain a blog. Not everyone is an aspiring DJ and feels comfortable podcasting.

Going where your market is is important.

Discover what works for you, what you feel comfortable with, and have the time and inclination to use. Then make sure you use at least one content tool, and at least one outreach tool. For example, a blog that you market with Twitter. But the more tools the better: their combined effect is greater than the sum of their parts.

Identify your calls to action

Calls to action are too often neglected in online marketing. You've gone to a lot of effort to get people onto your website – now tell them what you want them to do once they get there. Calls to action may include:

→ sign up to an email newsletter;

→ visit a website;

→ download a white paper;

→ become a fan on Facebook;

→ buy something;

→ enter a competition;

→ leave a comment.

Your main call to action on your website will often be to sign up to your email newsletter. Put this somewhere prominent, such as the top right-hand corner, which is where people tend to look first. You should also use calls to action in your email newsletter, and in your social media content. Again, a lot of time and effort has gone in to creating a video, a podcast or writing a blog post. What do you want people to do as a result of engaging with your content?

Using calls to action

Don't confuse people with too many calls to action, or they are likely to end up doing none of them. On your content tools, stick to just the one – and put it at the end. This includes at the end of blog posts, podcasts and videos. Why at the end? So that people can have a chance to see your content first and then decide if it's worth following up with a visit to a website, a download or a purchase. I've heard business podcasts that give listeners half a dozen things to do right at the beginning, before you've even heard the content – it's a real turnoff.

On social networks it is a little trickier: you don't want to annoy people with too many marketing messages. Stick to calls to action that offer something that your niche community is likely to be interested in, such as useful content. If you go off-topic, you will start to lose people. Add value and you will gain fans and followers. On Twitter, it's fine to include the occasional relevant promotional tweet, especially if it includes a time-limited discount code for your followers, but make your focus and the majority of your tweets useful news, information and links related to your industry. At least 80 per cent of your social networking updates should be useful information – and no more than 20 per cent marketing messages.

Measure your results

It is important to pause and evaluate your social media marketing at regular intervals to find out if it has all been worth it. Decide on what metrics you will use at the start of the process. Setting some goals for your results can be helpful too, but bear in mind that the numbers you can expect will vary considerably depending on how broad or narrow your topic is.

It can also take time, so don't give up too soon. Online marketing requires patience and a long-term approach. Having said that, don't be afraid to drop something that clearly isn't working. You will get better at evaluating what works the more you do, as you build up a number of campaigns that you can benchmark against.

There is an increasing number of measurement tools that you can use – some free and some that you pay for – and a lot you can do yourself. I recommend recording your key metrics on a monthly spreadsheet. Most webstat services will also send you a monthly report by email.

Ten ways to measure your success

1 **Web analytics**. There's a lot you can tell from your standard webstats package such as Google Analytics or Clicky Analytics. Not just about the number of visitors to your website, but the sources of that traffic and popularity of your content. Which social networks are driving the most traffic to your site? Which blog posts get the most views? It might be a good idea to write more of those.

2 **Email metrics**. How many people opened your email, and which links did they click on? Your email service provider (ESP), such as MailChimp, will provide detail on all this and more.

3 **Bean counting**. How many Facebook fans, Twitter followers and LinkedIn connections do you have? How many people have viewed your YouTube video? How many downloaded your podcast? How many people have subscribed to your blog's RSS feed? These are fairly bald numbers, but useful nonetheless.

4 **Rankings**. Where does your blog rank on Technorati or blogrankings.com? Where does your Twitter account sit in relation to other people in your industry on WeFollow? Where does your website rank on Alexa? Use rankings to compare yourself against your competitors.

5 **Platform-specific metrics**. Every social network in this book has one or more platform-specific metrics – either built in or available as a third-party service. Look at the end of each chapter for guidance on these.

6 **Calls to action**. How many people actually answered that call to action? If you only made it in one place, on one channel, you know what proportion of readers/followers/members did as you asked.

Get Up to Speed with Online Marketing

7 **Discount codes**. Create different discount codes for different social networks and other places you promote something.

8 **Surveys**. A more traditional method, but you can do some market research on the impact and awareness of your campaigns. Create an online survey with SurveyMonkey and promote it via your social networks.

9 **Conversational index**. This applies to blogs, and is a measure of the level of engagement with your content. It is the number of comments divided by the number of blog posts – and you're aiming for a figure above 1.

10 **Tracking links and unique landing pages**. OK, so 1,000 people watched your YouTube video. Your call to action was a web address for people to visit for more information. But how many took action? If you include a web address at the end of the video, and make it a unique URL – a specific web address that is only ever mentioned on that piece of video, but which automatically refers on to where you actually want people to land – you can see from your webstats exactly how many people not only watched the video, but took action.

By using a combination of these measures and setting a regular evaluation schedule, you can find out what works for you, and do more of it.

Manage the workload

We will look at ways to manage the workload for each tool, but if you follow these general principles, you will be able to avoid working all hours like a social media Stakhanovite:

1 **Aggregate** – rather than updating multiple sites all the time, link your accounts to leave a digital footprint in several places with a single action. For example, link your Pinterest account to Twitter and Facebook, so that each pin is shared on these networks.

2 **Automate** – for example, automatically tweet your blog using Twitterfeed.

3 **Integrate** social media into your working life with social media dashboards such as HootSuite and TweetDeck, and do updates on the move with social media smartphone apps.

4 **Audit** your existing social media, plan your resources, and reuse and repurpose material where possible.

5 **Invite** user-generated content, whether Flickr photos, video responses on YouTube, blog comments or guest posts.

6 **Share** the workload with multi-author blogs, and multiple logins and admins for Facebook pages or Twitter accounts.

7 **Schedule** Facebook and Twitter updates for the month ahead by using HootSuite, or write several blog posts in one session and schedule them to publish at later dates.

Finally, don't be afraid to ask for help if you need it. There are online tools to help you do that too, which we will look at in Chapter 16.

Once you have read this book, you will be in a better position to choose which tools you think will work for you, and to specify some calls to action. The rest of this book will look at the most important online marketing tools at your disposal, starting with the foundation of all your online marketing: your website.

Take action

→ **Define** your marketing goals. Write down your primary marketing aim and a specific marketing objective.

→ **Search** for your community of interest and fill in the 'Our community can be found at:' part of your marketing plan.

→ **Choose** three to five tools that you think you will want to use in your marketing. Include at least one content tool and at least one outreach tool.

→ **Identify** a call to action for each tool you choose.

→ **Decide** what metrics you will use for each tool to measure your success.

→ **Read on** to discover more about these tools, and choose the right ones for you!

Get online

Part Two

Establish a web presence

How to build a website with no technical knowledge

Chapter Three

A website is the most important marketing tool for your business – if you do nothing else from this book, you absolutely must have a website. Fortunately it is much easier to establish a web presence than it used to be. There's no need to put this off for a lack of geeky coding experience: whether you hire a web developer or build it yourself with an easy-to-use content management system (CMS), creating and maintaining websites is more straightforward than ever. You can even add sophisticated functions using low-cost third-party tools rather than having these coded into your website. And once you have your website, don't forget to spread the word with social media to draw people on to it. The web is about connecting people, and your website is about connecting them to your business.

Creating and maintaining websites is more straightforward than ever.

What is a website?

It is no longer sufficient to have a website to say you have an online presence – you also need to be present where your customers spend their time online, such as Facebook and Twitter. But a website is your essential starting point. The aim of all your other online marketing activities is to drive people to it, but it must also point outward to your presence elsewhere on the internet. It is the hub of your online marketing activities. The other point of your website is to sell your products or services. Once you've gone to the trouble of getting people on to your website, you want to sell them something! Make your website your online point of sale. Your market, your business and its needs will determine what sort of website you go for. Some options are:

→ A **brochure website**. Websites used to be static collections of pages that happened to be published online, but might just as well have been printed. Today we expect more from a website than uploaded business stationery. We expect dynamic, ever-changing content. A brochure site will establish a web presence for you – but it's not going to get you as many leads as a dynamic website.

→ A **blog**. A blog is really just a special kind of website that you can update yourself – not just posts that are regularly updated, but pages that are more static. This means you can use blogging software such as WordPress as a content management system (CMS) to build an entire website. Whether your main business website is a blog or a traditional brochure website, the principles in this chapter apply to the content and approach of your site. We will look in more detail at blogging in Chapter 6.

→ An **e-commerce site**. This is a website that is set up to sell products and take payments online. It is no longer necessary to invest a small fortune in creating a bespoke e-commerce site with your own shopping cart function coded from scratch. There is e-commerce software you can use on your site, and most CMS have ecommerce plugins available. It is now acceptable for any business to use PayPal to take payments on their websites without looking 'unprofessional'. You can even sell your products through an Ebay or Amazon store that you link to from your website.

Why a website is essential for business

A website is the most important marketing tool for your business. An online presence is a minimum requirement if you want to present a professional image, reach new customers and increase profits. A website:

→ is a 'shop window' that works for you 24 hours a day;

→ enables you to reach a global market;

→ promotes your products and services;

→ gives you credibility;

→ offers online support to your customers (which can save you time);

→ provides a way for people to contact you.

Your clients and customers expect you to be online. How many times have people asked you for your web address, or said that they'll Google you? If you're not online, you don't exist. And they'll go to your competition, who *are* online.

Websites in action

How a Canadian marine electronics shop launched an ecommerce site

Roton (**www.roton.ca**) is a small business in Vancouver, Canada, that sells marine electronics. It has been outfitting sail and power boats with navigation, communication and entertainment equipment for over 35 years. It decided it needed to upgrade its static website to a fully functioning ecommerce store, and called in local web designer Pixelmade. Roton now sells over 500 products online, and can manage all inventory and web content itself.

Rather than start from scratch, the new site was created with a content management system (CMS) called Drupal, and is integrated with PayPal for secure transactions and Google Analytics to track visitor behaviour. Together with Search Engine Optimisation (SEO – see next chapter), the new site resulted in 240 per cent increase in traffic within three months of launch – and a boost to sales thanks to an online store that is open for business 24 hours a day.

Get the idea: Whether you're doing it yourself or hiring a designer, you don't need to have an ecommerce site coded from scratch. Use PayPal plus a CMS such as Drupal, Joomla, Powa or WordPress, using an ecommerce plugin where necessary. Then you can update and manage all web pages and product inventory yourself – and open for business online.

Source: **www.pixelmade.com/small-business-web-design-vancouver**

Get up to speed with your website

So, how do you build a website with no technical knowledge? The short answer is you either hire a web designer, or build it yourself using a CMS such as WordPress. But doing it yourself isn't for everyone, or suitable for every website. And there are other steps to think through. Do you have your own unique web address (domain name)? What content are you going to put on your website? How will you structure it? What functions can you add using third-party tools? These are the steps you need to take:

→ Choose a domain name.

→ Write a design brief.

→ Plan your content.

→ Extend your website's functionality with third-party tools.

→ Get social: build connections and community.

Doing it yourself isn't for everyone.

Choose a domain name

It looks far more professional to have a proper email address on your business cards, such as joe@xyzwidgets.com rather than, say, xyzwidgets@gmail.com. For this you need a domain name, which you can use for your website too. It is fine to start off just using it for email, before your website is ready (though people might come looking for it), but you must secure the domain name you want as soon as you can, before someone else takes it.

There are very many companies out there selling domain names and web hosting: **www.godaddy.com**, **www.heartinternet.co.uk** and **www.123-reg.co.uk** are popular, but do a search for one that suits you. Domain names and hosting are relatively cheap. Unless you're using a hosted service, such as **http://wordpress.com**, you will also need some web space to host your site at. The simplest way is to use the same company for both your hosting and domain name registration.

Frequently asked questions

Should I hire a web designer or do it myself?
Unless web design is your specialism, it's rarely worth having a go yourself, and not worth your time to learn how to code websites. The exception to this is if you set up your website using a CMS such as WordPress, which can be a good way to set up a professional-looking web presence quickly. If your website requires a lot of complex functionality, don't try this at home: hire a designer. There is advice on how to find someone in Chapter 16. But take a look first at some third-party tools, as there may be an off-the-shelf solution you can use.

Create your business site in minutes using WordPress

The quickest way to get a professional-looking website if you don't already have one is to put down this book right now and sign up for an account at **http://wordpress.com**.

Don't want to commit to a regular online diary? You can also use blogging software such as WordPress as a CMS to create 'traditional' websites, since you can add and update pages as well as blog posts. Want to update some of your web content? No need to call your web developer – just do it yourself with an easy-to-use interface. Write some text, add some links, upload some images, click 'Publish' and you're done. It really is that easy.

Using free tools such as WordPress it is actually easier to build a dynamic business website than the most basic static brochure site coded from scratch. There are two versions of WordPress: **http://wordpress.com**, which is hosted on their servers and requires no technical knowledge – you can be up and running in about 15 minutes; and **http://wordpress.org**, which you need some technical skills to use as you need to download the software and upload it to your own server. We will look more at the pros and cons of each in Chapter 6.

Write a design brief

The starting point for your website is your design brief. You should think this through and put some ideas down on paper before contacting a web designer or developer. The questions below are the sorts of things they will ask. And even if you're doing it yourself, it's still a good discipline to go through this process. It will help you stay focused on the core aims and marketing objectives of your site. Think of it as a mini business plan for your website.

The starting point for your website is your design brief.

Things to consider include:

1 **What type of website do you want**? E.g. a simple online brochure, an ecommerce site, a business blog?

2 **What is the main purpose of your website**? What are its marketing aims and objectives?

3 **What look and feel are you after**? Should it follow a specific brand image or colour scheme? Which sites do you like the look and feel of? Who is your competition? What are their sites like?

4 **Who is your target audience**? E.g. specific business sectors, individuals, current clients, prospective clients? Are you selling to other businesses or to consumers?

5 **What is your main 'call to action'**? What do you want people to do once they arrive at your website?

6 **How many pages will your website have**? E.g. home, about, contact, services, products, individual product pages, clients, news, etc. How will the site be structured?

7 **What functionality do you need**? E.g. a 'contact us' form, shopping cart functions, online booking system?

8 **Do you already have images** or do you need your designer to source these?

9 **What media do you require**? E.g. audio, video, Flash animation?

10 **What is your schedule**? Do you have a critical launch date, e.g. to coincide with a product launch or marketing campaign?

Other things to bear in mind when hiring a designer/developer:

→ Although I use the terms 'web designer' and 'web developer' fairly interchangeably, I would usually expect the former to be able to do some graphic design work and the latter to be more of a coder. What can yours do for you? Will you have to hire a graphic designer separately to come up with a graphic design concept?

→ How will the process work? Will the site just be uploaded when it is finished and you have approved it? Or will it be an iterative process that you can comment on while it is in development?

→ Can your web developer ensure your site will look good not just on a range of web browsers but on a range of devices, such as smartphones and iPads? Will the site adjust itself to fit the device it is being viewed on (often known as 'responsive web design')? This matters more than ever now that so many people access the internet in this way.

Plan your content

Even if you are putting pages together on a content management system, it pays to spend a bit of time first planning what content you want, and how you want it structured. What will your main pages be? What subpages? What content will appear on each?

Information architecture

A useful starting point is an information architecture (IA) diagram – a simple flowchart showing what goes where. You can do this as a simple sketch on a piece of paper. Figure 3.1, for example, gives a simple IA diagram for an imaginary image consultancy business.

It's a good idea to keep your information architecture shallow – i.e. don't give people too many layers to click through to get to key information. It should be easy and intuitive for people to get to your content quickly and easily. For a complex site, you might want to run your IA past a few people in your target market to make sure it makes sense.

FIGURE 3.1 Information architecture

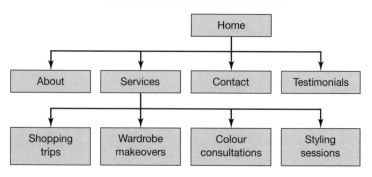

Key pages to consider for your website include:

Home page: This should provide information about what you can offer your customers or clients, plus a brief overview of what else they can find on your site. Think also about your main call to action; make any special offers prominent on the home page and, if it is a selling site, make it easy to get to your product catalogue.

About us: Tell your customers a bit about yourself, your business and its history, and your vision. If your business is closely linked to you personally, be sure to include a brief biography and headshot, plus links to your personal presence elsewhere on the internet, such as your personal blog, Twitter account or Facebook profile.

Contact us: Make it easy for people to reach you. Provide contact information in the footer of each page, with more detail on a dedicated Contact page. Include your mailing address, phone number and email address as a minimum. You may also want to include a contact form.

Products/Services: A summary page of what you can offer, plus links to pages for individual products or services. Think about a call to action for each of these pages – such as a prominent 'buy now' button. See also **Shop** below.

Pricing: This depends on what business you're in. If you're selling physical products, include clear pricing, and ideally a currency converter if you're selling internationally. It is not always so easy to price services online, but you could consider listing a range or minimum price if appropriate, such as '£50 +VAT per hour', 'from €650' or 'between $1,500 and $2,000'.

Search: Include a search box prominently on your site so that visitors can look for the things they're interested in. If you're using WordPress, this function will be included. You can also add a Google custom search box to your site by going to **www.google.com/cse** and cutting and pasting the code.

Shop: This might be a significant part of your site if your business sells products online, or a single page if you have just a few products you sell. Use PayPal 'buy now' buttons if you don't have many products, and consider more ambitious ecommerce options if you have a large store.

Testimonials/Reviews: Include testimonials from current customers to show that you have a proven track record of delivering real benefits rather than theoretical ones. It helps reassure potential new clients. If you don't have any testimonials yet, email your clients and ask for feedback or use LinkedIn to solicit recommendations. If you sell physical products, include product reviews.

Frequently asked questions (FAQs): These can help your customers learn more about what you do, your products and services, and help you spend less time answering queries by phone or email. If you have a complicated product, consider including online video demonstrations or tutorials somewhere on your site.

Press room: If you regularly deal with the media, send out press releases, or get requests for interviews or speaking, include a virtual press room on your website. This should include your press releases, a high-resolution headshot and 100-word biography of you and any other colleagues who might appear in the media, a paragraph of blurb about your business, and examples of any media appearances or press coverage. Include a list of topics you speak on or would be happy to be interviewed about.

Event calendar: If you regularly run events, such as seminars, product launches or demonstrations, or exhibitions, include an event calendar so that customers know when you are coming to a town near them. A calendar is also useful if you make regular client visits. Savile Row tailor Thomas Mahon uses one on his **www.englishcut.com** website to publicise his US trips. Likewise, tailors King and Allen list their 'fitting days' all over the UK at **www.kingandallen.co.uk**.

Blog: Your website may include a blog as a subsection (e.g. **www.mybusiness.com/blog**) or link to a blog on a separate domain name, or your entire site may be a blog, with the latest posts appearing on the front page. If your blog is separate from your main site, you can still pull in extracts of your latest couple of blog posts on to your home page to highlight your blog and to keep your content fresh.

Newsletter: There are a couple of options here:

→ A **Latest News** section on your site can be driven by blogging software even if you don't want a blog per se. You can also deliver the latest news posts automatically by email using a service called Feedburner (**www.feedburner.com**).

→ An **email newsletter** goes one stage further, and if you make it exclusive to subscribers you can include special offers and discounts that only apply to newsletter recipients.

Resources: Share some useful content in your field of expertise, such as market reports, white papers or other documents that can be downloaded for free, or in exchange for signing up to your email newsletter. Use these as an opportunity to position yourself as an expert and share useful information without too much of a hard sell.

Site map: For a large site with many subpages, a site map can help people find the information they need. It should be set out as a list of text links, with subpages indented.

Legal boilerplate: Familiarise yourself with any statutory requirements in your territory. These may include listing your company name, address and registration number. If you are based in the EU, a controversial new 'cookie law' means that you need to ask site visitors to consent to the use of cookies on your website, if your site uses them, and direct visitors to your privacy policy. There are WordPress plugins that will do this for you. Whether or not this applies to you, it is good practice anyway to include a privacy policy that explains what data you collect and how you use it. It is also a good idea to include an accessibility statement to inform visitors of the accessibility standards your site meets, what steps you are taking to improve them, and how people can report any accessibility concerns to you.

Extend your website's functionality with third-party tools

Why reinvent the wheel? Do you really need your own, bespoke, lovingly hand-coded web form, shopping cart or event booking system? There was a time when you had to do it all yourself because it looked more professional and things like PayPal didn't exist. Today, even large organisations use third-party web services to fulfil key, specialised functions of their businesses online. They do it better and cheaper than you could yourself. And nobody minds any more – these sites are trusted and can actually make you look more professional than if you attempt it yourself. Most are easy to use and will provide you with a bit of code that you just need to copy and paste into your website or CMS.

They do it better and cheaper than you could yourself.

Here are some third-party websites and services to consider for your business:

1 **PayPal** (**www.paypal.com**). What did we do before PayPal? There is no longer any need to develop complex credit card merchant scripts on your website to sell things online. In fact, it is better not to, since PayPal is a more trusted and more secure way of taking payments online. Other online payment solutions include Google Checkout, ClickBank and WorldPay.

2 **Ecommerce software. E-Junkie** (**www.e-junkie.com**) is a web-based service that provides 'shopping cart' and 'buy now' buttons, and is suitable for both physical products and digital downloads. For digital downloads such as ebooks, it will sort out the delivery of files for you; for physical products it will calculate shipping and manage inventory. **Powa** (**www.powa.com**) is another web-based service that enables you to create a branded, professional online store without technical knowledge – but will also help you find a designer if you need something more bespoke. Other ecommerce solutions are based on installing software on your own site, including **Actinic** and **ZenCart**. If you use WordPress for your site, Premium WordPress theme provider WooThemes (**www.woothemes.com**) also offers an ecommerce plugin called **WooCommerce**.

3 **Wufoo** (**http://wufoo.com**). If you need a form or questionnaire embedding in your website, particularly if you want to collect payments at the same time with PayPal, use Wufoo. Useful if you want clients to brief you on a project online – and pay you in advance at the same time – or for taking orders or event registrations.

4 **Eventbrite** (**www.eventbrite.com**). Many organisations who once sold tickets on their own website are now using Eventbrite. It is probably the best-known web service for promoting events and selling them online. Add details of your event, set the pricing, and you're good to go. Customers can pay online, by linking to your PayPal account – or they can request a traditional invoice.

5 **Google Maps** (http://maps.google.com). If you want to include a map of your business on your Contact page, why not make it an interactive Google map? Instead of a static map, visitors can zoom in and out, find directions, use Google Streetview where available, and even review your business.

6 **BbPress** (http://bbpress.org). Simple and elegant forum software from the creators of WordPress. Use it to set up discussion forums inside your WordPress.org site.

Third-party web tools enable you to offer a much wider range of services than you could yourself. The subscription fees involved are modest compared to the time and money you would spend on building your own web functions – and some are free. Their level of specialism and ease of use make these tools compelling, and provide a better experience for your customers than you could build yourself.

Get social: build connections and community

Dynamic, changing content will make you look more up to date, and more popular with search engines. Compelling content will keep people coming back for more. Third-party tools will extend your functions. But to really engage your clients and customers, you need to go where they are and start conversations with them.

Compelling content will keep people coming back for more.

In the relatively recent old days of 'web 1.0', businesses would put all their online marketing efforts into their website – if they even had one. Now this is an area where the 80/20 rule applies. Only 20 per cent of your online marketing time should be spent on your core business website. The other 80 per cent should be spent on your blog, your Facebook page, your Twitter feed, and other social sites. It should be spent connecting with people, creating community, and raising awareness of your brand. This 'off-site' activity will draw people on to your website – but it is far more productive to engage with people there than on your own site.

This is what makes your website a marketing hub: at the centre of the spokes that lead out to a variety of social sites. Spend time building your site, getting it right, and making sure it has all the key functions you need to do business – and keep it up to date – but then get out there, get social, and grow your business!

Measure your results

Website analytics

Your webstats, or web analytics, are the primary means by which you will measure the effectiveness of your website. All services available run on the same principle: you sign up for an account, tell it which website(s) you want to track, and it gives you some code to include on all the pages you want it to track. This is usually a simple matter of adding the code to your 'footer' file and uploading it. Be aware that using any analytics service is likely to involve the use of 'cookies', meaning that, if you are based in the EU, you will need to gain consent for this from your site visitors. The two most popular webstats services are:

→ **Google Analytics (www.google.com/analytics)**. This is the most popular service, used on around 55 per cent of the 10,000 most popular websites. It is free to use for up to 50 sites – so long as each site has fewer than five million page views per month or is linked to an AdWords campaign (see next chapter).

→ **Clicky Analytics (www.clicky.com)**. This is free to track one site, and then there are payment plans for up to 10 or 30 sites. The 10-site 'Pro' plan costs $80 or about £55 per year – unless you choose the 'Pro Plus' premium features including heatmaps, when it goes up to $120 or £80. I've used Clicky for a while – initially because it was the only service to offer real-time stats, but also because it seemed good at tracking traffic from social sites.

Get Up to Speed with Online Marketing

Website rankings

You can also measure where your site ranks by signing up to Alexa (**www.alexa.com**) or the Google Toolbar, which includes the Google PageRank bar. You can also look at the rankings for any website – including your competitors'.

→ **Alexa internet**. Download their toolbar from **www.alexa.com/toolbar**. Once installed, the toolbar collects data on browsing behaviour which is sent back to the website where it is stored and analysed and is the basis for their web traffic reporting. You can use the toolbar to see how popular a website is and how many sites are linking to it. Alexa rankings are often quoted to illustrate how popular a website is – for example, for some while now the top three sites in the world have been Google, Facebook and YouTube in that order (which is why it's a good idea to have a presence on these sites!).

→ **PageRank**. This the Google algorithm that expresses Google's view of the importance of a particular web page as a score out of 10, and is partly determined by the number of incoming links. Google interprets a link from page A to page B as a 'vote' for page B. But the strength of that vote also depends on how important Google considers page A to be.

Inbound links

You can get a measure of your incoming links from your webstats and Alexa, and also use your webstats to see what search terms people are using to find you. Your WordPress dashboard should also record incoming links.

For something more comprehensive, simply type **link:yourdomain. com** into a Google search to pull up a list of web pages that link to your domain. If you want to go a stage further than this, sign up for a free Google Webmaster account (**www.google.com/webmasters**) to gain more insights, and a greater range of inbound links, including 'nofollow' links that don't contribute to the authority ranking of your website in Google searches.

Web design best practice

1 **Don't spend a fortune**. Consider doing it yourself with WordPress.

2 **Don't reinvent the wheel**. Use third-party tools rather than develop complex features from scratch.

3 **Plan your site**. Use a design brief to plan your website, even if you are doing it yourself.

4 **Accessibility**. Be aware of accessibility issues when designing your site and adding content – not least because it is a legal requirement to make your site accessible in some jurisdictions, e.g. the UK where the Disability Discrimination Act comes into play. Will your site be accessible to people with a visual impairment, for example, who may use screenreader software to consume your content? Use alt tags to describe images, and keep key navigation links towards the top of your site. See the Web Accessibility Initiative (WAI) for more information: **www.w3.org/WAI**.

5 **Usability**. Does your site work on all major browsers? What about mobile devices? Test it on multiple platforms so you don't get any nasty surprises. Does the 'user interface design' (UID) work? That is, does the design make the user's interaction as simple and efficient as possible, in terms of enabling them to accomplish what they want to do (and what you want them to do) on your site? Do some usability testing – even if that is just asking a few friends to perform a specific task on your site and watching them do it. This can be quite enlightening – especially if they struggle with something that seems obvious to you!

Take action

→ **Secure** a domain name for your business.

→ **Decide** whether to hire a designer or do it yourself.

→ **Set up** your business website.

→ **Plan** your design brief and content.

→ **Extend** your functionality with third-party sites.

→ **Focus** on building connections and community on social sites.

Boost your search engine rankings

How to increase your visibility on Google

Chapter Four

Now that you've built your website, people won't necessarily come. Not if they can't find you. And the main way people find you online is still via search engines. Without a website, you don't exist. Without a search strategy, you exist but you're invisible. Google isn't the only search engine – others are available, notably Bing and Yahoo! But Google is so big it has become a verb – and has a massive market share. It made the news when, at the end of 2012, Google's market share in the UK dipped below 90 per cent for the first time in five years – largely due to its main rival, Microsoft's Bing, increasing its share to 5 per cent.

> **Without a website, you don't exist. Without a search strategy, you exist but you're invisible.**

Nor is Google the only way people search for what they want online. People also search on Facebook, Twitter, YouTube and other social sites they spend so much time on. Much of the rest of this book will help you to be found on these sites too, but being on these sites will also make you more visible on Google. And, of course, the social network that will make you most visible on Google is now its own: Google+ (see Chapter 14).

The principles in this chapter apply to all search engines, but we will pay particular attention to improving your visibility in Google.

What is search engine marketing?

How Google works

Google is the world's largest search engine. It does two things:

1 Crawls the internet looking for web pages, and indexes them in a vast catalogue. It is no longer necessary to manually submit websites to Google – it happens automatically. Google will find your pages via incoming links from websites that are already indexed. This is one reason why you want other sites to link to yours. You can also manually submit your site at **www.google.com/addurl** if you want. This is the easy part.

2 Decides which are the best pages – both the best match for a search query, and the ones that have the best rank. Getting your pages to rank highly is the harder part, and is what search engine marketing (SEM) will achieve for you.

The decision-making algorithm that decides which pages are the best is based on two things: relevance and authority. The relevance of a page to the search query is simply based on the keywords used to perform a search. But since there are likely to be hundreds of thousands of pages that match, Google then ranks them in order of authority, using its PageRank algorithm.

This algorithm is based on work done at Stanford University on how to measure the authority of academic papers. The simple answer is: citations. The more a paper is cited by other papers, the more authority it has. But not all citations are equal: a citation from a paper that itself has a lot of citations carries more weight than a citation from one that has few or none.

This is exactly how the Google PageRank algorithm works. The more links there are from other websites to your website, the more authority your website has. But not all incoming links are equal: an incoming link from a website that itself has a lot of incoming links carries more weight than an incoming link from one that has few or none.

How search engine marketing works

Online marketing is all about making your stuff easy to find. Search engine marketing is about making your stuff easy to find on Google and other search engines, by increasing the position of your placement on search engine results pages (SERPs). This is done via three methods:

1 Search engine optimisation (SEO) – i.e. making your website more attractive to Google.

2 Paid placements – e.g. using Google AdWords.

3 Attracting in-bound links – e.g. using article marketing.

The good news is that the first of these methods – SEO – is not only free but it is also more effective. If you can increase your natural or organic search engine rankings, i.e. without paying for them, people are more likely to click on them. Research shows that 75 per cent of people using Google click on the natural search results, and 25 per cent on the paid-for ads.

Google AdWords is still worth a look, though, and needn't cost a fortune. Your paid-for listings become cheaper and more effective the more specific to your business the search terms you choose are. Search engine marketing is affordable even for small businesses.

Part of the aim of your SEM is to get incoming links from high-authority sites, in order to increase your authority and therefore your position on SERPs. We will therefore also take a look at article marketing in this chapter. This involves submitting content to high-ranking article sites such as Ezine (**http://ezinearticles.com**) in order to drive traffic back to your site and increase your credibility by positioning you as an expert in your field – but also to increase your authority with Google.

Blogs in particular really help push up your search engine rankings.

Like so much in the online marketing world, one of the best ways to encourage links to your website is to create great content. The content tools we will look at in Part 3 will help you create content for your website and for other social sites. Blogs in particular really help push up your search engine rankings.

Why search engine marketing works for business

How many times have you looked for something on Google today? How many other people out there are searching right now for products or services exactly like the ones you offer? How many will find your website? Most people don't get past page one of the search engine results delivered by Google. Getting a high placement on this page is critical to driving search engine traffic to your site.

A high placement can be paid for (though Google still selects the results it thinks will be most appropriate to the person searching, to maintain its own credibility), or achieved for free through SEO and getting links from high-authority sites.

For example, if you've just launched your website for your catering business and no one is linking to it yet, Google assigns a low authority to your pages. If you then start a blog, each post is a new page for Google to index. Food bloggers may find you and start linking to your blog posts. This will increase your authority and your position on Google. Then if a site such as the *Observer Food Monthly* website happens to have links to your site, your authority will skyrocket, since this site is a high-ranking website with lots of incoming links.

Google is a global site, but your business doesn't have to be global to benefit from it. People can choose to restrict search results to their own country for a start. But what if you're really local, and only really serve your local community? What if you're, say, a plumber who wants to focus on local work in your own town and the surrounding area? The traditional marketing approach would be to advertise in the local paper, and perhaps print leaflets and go out putting them through your neighbours' doors.

Google is a global site, but your business doesn't have to be global to benefit from it.

But a plumber is the sort of service you only need when you need it – it is not an impulse purchase. This means that you have to do repeat advertising every week in the local paper, and regular leaflet drops in order to get your phone number in front of your potential customers when they need you. That's going to be expensive.

If instead you have a website, people can Google you – the first port of call for many of us when we need a service. Make sure the locations you serve are on your website, so that searches for 'plumber Oxford' (or wherever) come up. Google Places makes this even easier. If I simply search for 'plumber', Google supplies the page shown in Figure 4.1.

Now, there are almost 10 million results for such a common word, as you might expect. But Google has learned that I live in Woking, and has supplied the top seven search results nearest to me, and shown them on an interactive map. For this reason, if you are a local business you *must* list yourself on Google Places. It's free to do this at **www.google.com/local/add**.

FIGURE 4.1 Google search engine results page

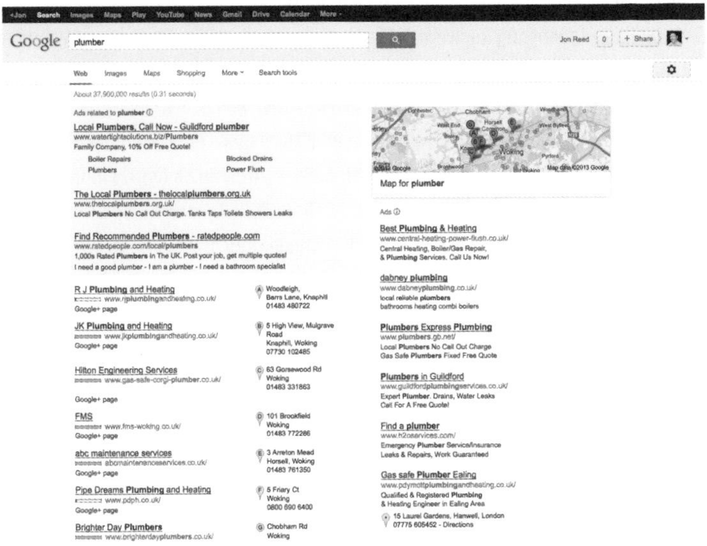

Note that the top three search results, with shading behind them, and the eight results in the right-hand column, are paid-for Google Ads. This is indicated by the heading 'Ads'. The rest are location-based, followed by natural, or organic, search results. Unsurprisingly, a Wikipedia definition is top of this list, since Wikipedia is such a high-authority site with lots of incoming links.

Search engine marketing in action

How an electrical services company doubled traffic and leads in weeks with SEO

Brda Electric, Inc. (**www.brdaelectric.com**) is a family owned and operated electrical services company in St Louis, Missouri, USA, that provides commercial and residential electrical services. Their sales leads and web traffic were once generated mainly by customer referral. Their website did not rank well for search terms and, as a result, did not generate new sales leads, meaning they were missing out on a lot of potential business.

Working with local internet marketing firm Terrakon Marketing, they gave the site a facelift and undertook extensive Search Engine Optimisation (SEO) work. This included identifying keyword phrases and optimising website copy, URLs, title tags, meta description tags and alt text on images.

As a result, their Google visitors doubled in a few weeks, website sales leads increased by two to four times, visitors spent a third more time on the website – and the website now ranks in the Google top five search results for 26 primary searches compared with just one previously. The site is now organically ranking for industry-competitive keywords – and the phone rings a lot more than before!

Get the idea: Spend some time auditing, assessing and optimising your website. This will pay dividends in terms of organic search engine rankings, which in turn will lead to more traffic – and more sales leads. Don't think that search engine marketing isn't for you just because you are a local business – Google is the first place many people will turn when they need local services such as electricians, plumbers or roofers.

Source: **www.terrakon.com/local-seo-case-study**

Get up to speed with search engine marketing

There are three things you can do to get your SEM off to a great start:

→ Optimise your website.

→ Create a Google AdWords campaign.

→ Submit an article to Ezine.

Optimise your website

Get a natural high for your search results, for free, simply by taking a bit of time to make sure your website is as optimised as possible for search engines. SEO had a bad name in the early days of the web, when it was too often thought of as tricking Google into giving you a high ranking. Well, Google is wise to that now, and will soon boot you off if you try any of those 'black hat' techniques such as hiding keywords invisibly on your website. Besides, that's not very authentic, is it? And you don't want traffic simply because you're top of the Google list – you want it because what you have to offer is *relevant* to what people are searching for. Google delivers the results that are the best match for its searchers, and you get visitors who are actually interested in buying from you. It's a win–win situation.

Make sure your website contains the right content and code for Google to know that your site is relevant.

The first step is to make sure your website contains the right content and code for Google to know that your site is relevant to people searching on certain keywords. Things to pay attention to are:

→ **Page titles** – give each page its own unique, descriptive title.

→ **Page descriptions** – these show up in Google search results rather than on your site, and provide more information about your site.

→ **URLs** – make sure they include keywords. Blogs are great for this as the title of a blogpost usually shows up in its URL.

→ **Website content** – think about the headings you use, the text you use as links (choose something descriptive rather than 'click here'), and tag your images with text that is visible to Google (but not to your visitors), so that it can 'see' them.

Find out more about optimising your site for search engines at **www.getuptospeed.biz/seo**.

Create a Google AdWords campaign

Google AdWords is an example of pay per click (PPC) advertising. Each time someone clicks on one of your ads that shows up on the Ads section of the Google results page, you pay a small fee. You may prefer to focus on boosting your natural search results for free with SEO. But it's worth trying Google AdWords, if only for short periods of time, particularly when you first launch your website and have no traffic, or whenever you launch a new product or service that you want to raise awareness of.

Sign up for an account at **http://adwords.google.com**, and start creating your first campaign. Choose your ad text, the keywords you want to target (i.e. which search queries do you want Google to display your ad in response to?), and decide what your maximum bid is for those keywords. You can choose how much you pay, and set a daily budget, but bear in mind that the whole system is a live auction, and someone may outbid you for a higher place, particularly with very popular, generic – and expensive – keywords. It is also possible that a keyword will suddenly become more popular, and the cost per click (CPC) will go up.

It makes sense to try to stick to more niche, specific keywords in your campaign for two reasons:

1 **It's more effective** – you will get more targeted traffic.
2 **It's cheaper** – common search terms are more expensive.

You get a very limited number of words for your ad – so choose them carefully! You can also set up multiple variations of the same ad, and test them against each other – Google will help you pick the best one with the metrics it provides.

You can also send people who click on your ad to a specific landing page, so you can measure its effectiveness. The URL doesn't have to match the home page URL shown on the ad – though it must be the same domain. In addition to textual ads, you can also opt for image ads in a variety of standard sizes, and even video ads.

The ads you create don't just show up in Google either. The flipside of Google AdWords is Google AdSense. That is an ad-serving service that enables anyone with a blog or website to earn a bit of cash by hosting contextually relevant Google ads on their pages. So your ads could show up on a wide variety of other sites too.

Frequently asked questions

How do I choose keywords for my campaign?
You could just come up with a list of which keywords you *think* people will use to find you, and include them in your AdWords campaign – as well as on your website. Most people take the products and services they offer as a starting point, and think of all the keywords and search terms associated with them, and ▶

then generate a list to use within the text of their website. But the other way you can do this is to research the search terms people most often use in relation to your product or service. One way of doing this is to enter your web address into the Google search-based keyword tool at **www.google.com/sktool**. This will come up with keyword suggestions for you, based on pairing the content on all your pages with actual search terms that people use on Google. It will output a list of keywords in order of search volume: an instant, up-to-date keyword list customised to your site. Once your website is up and running, another thing you can do is to look at your webstats to see what search terms people are using to find you – and then tweak your keywords if it seems appropriate. This keyword research can also help you improve your web copy, titles, descriptions and headings, plus suggest topics to blog about, all of which will improve your natural search results without costing you a penny.

Submit an article to Ezine

Part of your SEM strategy is to get more incoming links from high-ranking websites. One way to do this is to create great content that people will not only find via search and social media, but will also want to link to. You *can* also ask people to link to you – but I would advise against this. I get link requests all the time, mostly from people who haven't understood what I do. I treat them as spam and delete them.

> **Part of your SEM strategy is to get more incoming links from high-ranking websites.**

One way you might think you can create incoming links to your website is to comment on other people's blogs – particularly if they are high-ranking blogs or news sites – since you can usually enter your URL with your comment. While this can indeed be great for driving traffic to your website, I'm afraid it doesn't work for boosting your site's authority in Google's eyes. These links are not, after all, citations of your website by an independent third party, as PageRank intended – and Google knows it. To get around this issue, the 'nofollow' attribute for certain links was invented. When Google sees a 'nofollow' link, it

Get Up to Speed with Online Marketing

knows that the site owner doesn't want to endorse the site being linked to. This applies to most blogs.

An exception to this is article sites such as Ezine (**http://ezinearticles. com**) – sites that you can submit content to with a byline and a biography box with a ('dofollow') link back to your website. Ezine is a high-authority site, and links back to your site will increase your authority. People reproduce Ezine articles on their own blogs and websites – on the condition that they are reproduced in full with full credit to the author complete with byline, bio and link – so Ezine is used by both content creators and consumers.

A note of caution, though: please don't use these sites cynically by putting up poor quality articles with links. They are not just about link-building, and they shouldn't be thought of as an acceptable face of the old 'black hat' technique of link farms: they are also about sharing your knowledge, building your credibility and positioning you as an expert. Like blog comments, you should expect to get traffic as a result. Unlike blog comments, you will also get SEO credit for the links.

Quick win

Use social media to increase search engine placements

A blog is one of the best ways of increasing your search engine results: you create more pages for Google to index, and more content that people will want to link to (see Chapter 6). But since other social sites, such as Twitter and Facebook, are themselves high-ranking sites, why not create accounts for your business? If you can gain at least 25 Facebook fans, and if it's available, you can even have your own URL – such as **www.facebook.com/ publishingtalk**. A Google search for 'Publishing Talk' lists the site itself first – but the Twitter account, Facebook page and LinkedIn group also appear on page one of the results.

Don't underestimate the power of social media to help you to be found – not just on social media sites themselves, but within Google. Having a presence on social sites helps people to find your business, even if they don't use these sites themselves.

Measure your results

One way to measure the results of your SEM campaign is simply to look at your webstats and measure your web traffic. But your traffic is not entirely generated by Google – especially if you are using social media to drive people to your website – so you will need to dig a bit deeper into the stats.

→ You also get a load of stats and metrics with Google AdWords to help you find out what's working and what isn't, and to help you improve your campaigns. If you use unique landing pages with your Google Ads, you can also work out not only how much traffic is coming from your ads (which Google will tell you), but also how many visitors are converting into leads.

→ Search Google yourself, using some of your chosen keywords, and note your natural search engine placements. If you're not coming as high up the list as you'd like, do something about it.

→ You can also search Google for just the pages in your site, by entering **site:mybusiness.com**. This will tell you how many pages of your site are indexed by Google – and which pages have the highest authority, since these appear top of the list.

→ Finally, monitor the number of incoming links to your website. Part of your SEM strategy is to increase the number and quality of these, so this is something you should be vigilant about.

SEO best practice

1 **Optimise your website** so you benefit from 'natural' search engine placements.

2 **Use natural language** on your website and blog posts rather than trying to force in keywords.

3 **Optimise URLs** of your blog posts so they contain the category and title. In your WordPress.org dashboard choose **Settings** and **Permalinks**, then select **Custom Structure** and enter **/%category%/%postname%/**.

4 **Cap your budget** – don't spend a fortune on Google Ads. Set a daily budget and keep your keywords niche.

5 **Advertise at launch** – use Google Ads when you first launch something, such as a new product or website.

6 **List your local business** in the Google Local Business Center at **www.google.com/local/add**.

7 **Submit articles to Ezine** that focus on providing useful content.

Take action

→ **Optimise** your website for Google.

→ **Research** your keywords with **www.google.com/sktool**.

→ **Sign up** to Google AdWords and start your first campaign.

→ **Submit** an article to Ezine.

Engage with email

How to build an email list without annoying people

Chapter Five

If you think email marketing involves sending people unsolicited Viagra ads, think again. Email is a tried and tested method for reaching the right people online *and* persuading them to take action. You need very little technical knowledge to get started, since there are plenty of excellent third-party services you can use, such as MailChimp or Campaign Monitor, to handle everything from signup forms and email templates to managing mailing lists and measuring your results. This allows you to focus instead on your email marketing strategy: your marketing aims, who you will target, and what you will email them.

What is email marketing?

Email marketing is the online equivalent of direct mail. Although every email you send to a client or potential customer could be thought of as email marketing, it really means sending bulk emails to your email list, or part of your list, with aims that might include:

→ **building** your relationship with existing customers;

→ **encouraging** repeat business;

→ **acquiring** new customers;

→ **persuading** people to buy something.

When it is used *with permission* for building and maintaining relationships with your customers, email marketing is an efficient and powerful tool that needs to be part of your online marketing mix.

Why email marketing works for business

'Why bother with email in the social media age?', you may ask. 'I've built up a massive opted-in mailing list on Facebook and Twitter – can't I just use that?' Well, yes, that is one of your aims for using social sites. And if you haven't yet built up a following, you'll find out how to later (see Chapters 10–15).

But there are three important reasons why email is still central to your online marketing even if you market your business on social networks:

1 **You own the data**. What happens if you get booted off Facebook? It does sometimes happen, for no good reason. What if the entire social network you've been relying on goes under? If you've built up your own email list, these things aren't a problem, as you, rather than a third-party site, own the data. Yes, build up your following on social networks – but use social media to promote incentives for followers to convert to mailing list subscribers.

2 **It is a more appropriate sales channel**. Not everyone likes being sold to on social networks. You need to use them with caution, keep your message relevant, and not just spam a social network with 'buy my product' messages. We're much more used to email as a sales channel, however, and if we've given permission to be included on an email list, we expect to be sold to at least some of the time.

3 **Not everyone uses a social networking site**. And those who do don't necessarily log on every day. However, most people pick up their email every day. An email sits in your prospect's inbox until they take some sort of action – whether that is to open or delete it. It is harder to ignore than a tweet, which may rapidly disappear down your customer's timeline never to be seen again.

One of your key calls to action on the social media channels you use should be 'Sign up to our newsletter'.

Email marketing in action

How a holiday cottage company increased click-through rate by 500 per cent with personalised emails

cottages4you (**www.cottages4you.co.uk**) is the largest cottage holiday lettings brand in the UK, with a portfolio of over 10,000 properties. They wanted to create a personalised email campaign to help customers choose their next holiday. Working with their ESP (email service provider), Emailcentre (**www.emailcenteruk.com**), they used two tactics to achieve this:

▶

1   Customers were reminded about their last holiday with the following elements: inserting a picture and details of the cottage where they previously stayed, a subject line of '<title> <surname> – hand-picked just for you!', a call to action and headline of 'Where next after <last cottage name>?' This helped the email stand out amongst the clutter in customers' crowded inboxes.

2   A 'propensity model' was used to calculate the most suitable properties for each individual customer. This was based upon factors including previous destinations, home location and other attributes such as whether they have pets or children. This ensured each cottage was truly relevant, and not simply in the same region as their previous stay.

Using a service from emailcenter called Maxemail made this easy to implement, with its ability to quickly create highly personalised content based on a set of data files. The first mockup of the proposed campaign took less than an hour to set up, with the copy and design tweaks taking up the majority of the build time.

cottages4you were able to measure the improved engagement by comparing the click-through rate from the new personalised emails with the generic emails that were sent to the same people earlier that month. Compared to the generic newsletter the new personalised emails saw the number of unique people clicking through increase by 499 per cent. In fact, 77 per cent of the click-throughs were on the personal recommendations section of the email, demonstrating it was this in particular that increased engagement with the email. Booking revenue generated from the email achieved a 2,882 per cent return on investment.

Get the idea: Email is a personal medium, and works best with personalised messages. Think about individuals rather than simply segments, and ways you can tailor your message to make it specific and relevant. This will depend to an extent on the quality of your customer data and how it can be used by your ESP – but most enable some sort of segmentation. Use your email metrics to measure key results such as click-throughs, and compare against previous campaigns.

Source: **www.emailcenteruk.com/case-studies/cottages4you.php**

Get up to speed with email marketing

The main steps to follow are:

→ Choose an email service provider.

- → Build your list.
- → Plan your campaign.
- → Write your first email.

Choose an email service provider

Don't even think about using your own email account to send mass mailings. For one thing, it only takes a low percentage of people to classify your mail as junk to give you real problems, possibly including suspension of your email account. A professional email service provider (ESP) will help you comply with legal requirements, since they generally adopt best practices, such as double opt-in systems and 'unsubscribe' links in each email footer. These services will also help you manage and maintain your email list database, including enabling you to split it into segments for highly targeted campaigns. But the other huge advantage is the detailed reporting statistics that they provide, which would be almost impossible for you to replicate in-house. These include how many people have opened your email, and how many have clicked through to specific links you included in your email.

I personally think MailChimp is hard to beat – and it's free until you build up a large list or want to send a lot of emails, so a good one to get started with – but I know people who swear by aWeber. Take a look at the websites of some ESPs, review the features and pricing on offer, and pick one that fits your needs best. Popular ESPs include:

- → MailChimp (**www.mailchimp.com**);
- → AWeber (**www.aweber.com**);
- → Campaign Monitor (**www.campaignmonitor.com**);
- → dotMailer (**www.dotmailer.com**).

These services all work in a similar way:

1 Upload your email contact list if you have one already, and manage your lists and sublists via the service.
2 Create an email newsletter signup form – usually a simple matter of choosing which fields you want to include – then copy the code provided and paste it into your website or blog.

3 Choose a ready-made email template or design your own. The amount of customisation available varies with each ESP.

4 Create a 'campaign' – i.e. a specific mailing. Write your email, test it by sending to yourself, then send it to one of your lists or sublists.

5 Measure your results. Whichever service you choose will provide detailed metrics on who has received, opened, taken action and clicked through to specific links within your email.

Build your list

Now that you've got a service provider, complete with a database to hold all those email addresses, how are you going to populate it? I would advise against buying in a list. Apart from risking contravening the increasingly strict laws about email marketing, it is cheaper and more effective to build your own. Email marketing should be about building relationships with people who actually want to hear from you:

→ **Get permission**. The overriding principle is you *must* get permission. Effective email marketing is permission-based marketing – not spam. If someone signs up to your list, they know to expect email from you. They are more likely to be interested in your email, and it is less likely to end up in their spam folder. Ideally, use a double opt-in system. This sends an email to someone who has signed up to your newsletter asking them to click on a link to confirm their subscription.

→ **Create a signup form**. This is very easy – no knowledge of HTML is required. Whichever email marketing service you use, a standard feature is the generation of an email newsletter signup form that you can put on your website or blog. Just choose the fields you want, and copy and paste the code. You should also be provided with a simple web address that links to any signup form you create, which is useful for sharing a link to your signup form via social networks.

→ **Make 'Sign up to our newsletter' your number one call to action**. Your email newsletter signup form is the most important call to action on your website, and should be in a prominent position on your home page.

→ **Ask in person**. Whenever you take a business card from someone, whether a prospective client, someone you meet at a networking event, conference or trade show, ask them if you can add them to your newsletter. You can sign them up manually to your list so long as you have their permission. And if you use a double opt-in system, they can always change their mind.

→ **Provide an example**. To show prospective subscribers exactly what they are signing up to, include a link to your latest newsletter, or include an image of it on your newsletter page. At the very least you should indicate on the signup form, or the web page where you invite people to join your list, what sort of content you will be sending them and how often.

→ **Offer an incentive**. Create a white paper, a short ebook or other downloadable resource that your community will value. Give it away for free – or, rather, sell it for the price of an email address.

→ **Use social networks**. Promote your list on Twitter, Facebook, LinkedIn, Google+ – anywhere you have a following to convert followers to email signups. Promote your signup incentive rather than your list. For example I have used the following tweet to promote my list for **www.getuptospeed.biz**: 'Free 5-day email course: Plan Your Online Marketing (PDF marketing plan template + 5 email tutorials) http://bit.ly/pyom5' If you don't yet have a decent-sized following on social networks, you could use a Google Ad to kick-start things.

Frequently asked questions

What can I offer as an email signup incentive?

Creating signup incentives doesn't have to be too onerous a task – but they should be valuable enough for people to want to download them and directly relevant to the aims of the list you are using them to build. For example, I gave away a one-page PDF 'Twitter Cheat Sheet' that explains Twitter jargon to build a list with the aim of promoting a related ebook, *The Publishing Talk Guide to Twitter*. I built up this list before the ebook was even ready, by promoting it on the Publishing Talk blog and via social media, particularly Twitter, using a customised Bitly link: **http://bit.ly/pttcs**. This alerted people to the forthcoming book, gave them something to ▶

use in the meantime, and helped me build a sizable list of people who I knew were interested enough in Twitter resources to join the list. When the ebook came out, I mailed the list with a time-limited discount code. This is a method you can adapt to any industry. What cheat sheets or other downloadable resources would be useful to your community, build your list and warm up the sale of related products?

Plan your campaign

As with all of your marketing activities, decide on your objectives. Selling might be one of them – but it is not the only thing email marketing can be used for. Some of your emails may not be directly sales-related, but draw people on to your website or promote your products or services more indirectly. Your content and style may vary accordingly.

Decide on your objectives.

A 'campaign' in email marketing usually means a specific, single mailing. But it can also be used to describe your overall approach over a longer period of time. Types of email you might send include:

→ **Special offers**. A very common way to use email marketing, and an incentive for people to sign up to your list, is to make promotional offers available exclusively to subscribers. Use time-limited discount codes, and measure responses with click-throughs (as measured by your email marketing service), unique landing pages (as measured by your webstats) or simply by using a unique discount code for each campaign.

→ **Quick announcements**. Sometimes called postcard emails, these are brief announcements with a single call to action that might relate to a time-restricted sale or special offer.

→ **Video postcards**. Make a short video explaining your offer, or giving some useful information related to a product you might promote in a later campaign, as a way of 'warming up' the sale. Embed a still image that links to your video, ideally on a page on your website that invites them to watch the video and then take some further action.

→ **Customer surveys**. Surveys can be used to gain feedback on your service, or help develop new products while at the same time raising awareness of your new product. They are easy to set up using **www.surveymonkey.com**.

→ **Press releases**. If you have a discrete list of media contacts you've built up, this can be a useful way of distributing press releases with a view to getting media coverage. Include links to the virtual press room on your website.

→ **Autoresponder campaigns**. These are very powerful, will help you build your list, *and* save time. I use them a lot. Whenever someone signs up to a list for which I offer an incentive, such as free PDF sample pages from the latest edition of *Publishing Talk Magazine*, or whenever someone signs up to the magazine mailing list – they are sent an email (after confirming that they really do want to sign up) with a link to the download. Actually, in MailChimp terms, this is simply the 'Final Welcome Email' and not really an autoresponder. I do something a little more sophisticated with the email list for this book. This incentive is not only a PDF download (a marketing plan template), but a five-day email course on online marketing planning that explains how to use it. This is delivered in a series of email tutorials over a five-day period. See **www.getuptospeed.biz/ plan-your-online-marketing** for details. This is all managed automatically by MailChimp. Think about what might work in your industry. It doesn't have to be a series of email tutorials or a lot of content. I have seen business coaches use the same approach to email a series of short business tips over a series of days.

→ **Newsletters**. Possibly the most common form of email marketing is a regular newsletter that is sent to your entire list. An email newsletter is a 'softer' way of selling. It can be a powerful way of keeping in touch with your clients and customers without annoying them with constant sales messages. The purpose of an email newsletter is relationship building with previous, current and prospective clients. The focus is on providing useful information in their niche field of interest – a similar approach that you would adopt with a blog. You might even include some extracts from latest blog posts with a 'read more ...' link, in order to draw them on to your site. While the information is related to what you can offer, it is not a hard sell. It should, however, include a call to action.

Your newsletter may contain some or all of these:

➔ Useful information about your area of expertise.

➔ Latest news from your industry.

➔ Tips and 'how to' features.

➔ Upcoming events, conferences or trade fairs you will be attending.

➔ Special offers with discount codes exclusive to subscribers.

➔ Details of a new product you've launched and the key benefits it offers.

Write your first email

Keep your messages short and to the point, compelling, interesting and valuable. Make sure they are personalised, relevant to the list or subsection of the list you are sending it to, get the right message to the right person, and include a call to action. If you have several sections in your newsletter, consider using extracts and 'read more ...' links to direct them to the full article on your blog or website. Think carefully about the individual elements of your emails, particularly:

➔ **From**. Send email from a person. It is more likely to be opened if the email address is recognised as a real person by the recipient, ideally from someone they are already used to receiving email from.

➔ **To**. As with your 'from' field, all the emails in your database should be to a real person. Your email is unlikely to reach anyone if it is being sent to info@, sales@, etc.

➔ **Subject**. Grab attention, but avoid any words that might get trapped by a spam filter. These include 'FREE!'.

➔ **Body**. The general rule for HTML emails is a maximum width of 600px, but your ESP should handle any formatting, size and layout requirements. When it comes to composing your email, keep the information in short, bite-sized chunks with the most important information at the top of your email.

➔ **Call to action**. Don't confuse people with too many calls to action. If you can include one clear prominent call to action in each newsletter – perhaps a 'buy now' button, or a link to 'read more', 'take our survey', 'subscribe to our podcast' or whatever it may be – you are more likely to get click-throughs.

→ **Unsubscribe instructions**. Always be clear about how recipients can unsubscribe from your emails. Not only is this a requirement, it will maintain the value of your list. You don't want disinterested people taking up valuable room on your list. And without clear unsubscribe instructions, people will be tempted to hit the 'spam' button – even if they willingly signed up to your list. They may have forgotten, or just decided they no longer need the information. If too many people do this, your ESP may suspend your account until you can explain yourself. That is why I tend to put unsubscribe instructions at the *top* of my emails instead of in the footer.

→ **Footer**. Put in all your contact information so people can get in touch with you, and to meet any statutory requirements. The UK, for example, requires businesses to include their registered address and number on websites and emails as well as printed stationery.

Always send yourself a test email before mailing your entire list to make sure it looks as you intended and there are no glaring errors or omissions. Test the links to make sure they all go to the right place.

Quick win

Use FeedBurner to create an email newsletter from your blog

If you have a blog, it automatically comes with an RSS feed. That stands for 'Really Simple Syndication', and is simply a way for people to subscribe to your latest blog posts in a newsreader such as Google Reader. But if you manage your feed through FeedBurner (**www.feedburner.com**) you have additional options for the way you deliver your blog feed – including delivering latest posts by email. This means you can set up an ad-hoc email newsletter from your blog if you're not yet ready to take the plunge with one of the professional email marketing services.

→ Create a separate 'newsletter' category within your blog (which will generate its own RSS feed) – or consider your entire blog your newsletter.

▶

→ Use FeedBurner to create a feed – for your blog or for the discrete newsletter category you created.

→ On the FeedBurner site, click on the **Publicize** tab and then the **Email Subscriptions** link in the left-hand menu.

→ Two alternative pieces of HTML code are supplied: a signup form or a simple link. Use this on your blog or website.

→ Click the **Email Branding** link to choose the text and link colours your email will use, and the logo you want to appear on it.

→ To see the email addresses of people who have subscribed to your RSS feed by email, click the **Analyze** tab and the **See more about your subscribers** link. Scroll down, beneath the pie chart, to **Email Subscription Services**. Click on **FeedBurner Email Subscriptions** and then **Manage Your Email Subscribers List**. You will see a list of email addresses of people who have subscribed to your RSS feed. You can export these if you wish.

The advantages of this approach, if you already have a blog, is that it is an incredibly easy way to set up an email newsletter. The downside is that, although you have access to the list of email addresses, you can't send a message to them without creating a new blog post. This means you can't make special offers available to subscribers only – since everyone can see your newsletter on your blog. You also don't have access to the metrics you have with an email marketing service. This is really just an alternative way of delivering your latest blog posts to those who prefer to receive them by email instead of visiting your site. But it can be a useful halfway house between a blog and a newsletter. It is certainly a great way of promoting your blog.

Manage the workload

Ideally you will send newsletter emails monthly. Plan them in advance, and consider theming them around specific topics, either related to your industry or to seasonal events and promotions such as New Year Offers, Valentine's Day, Spring Cleaning or Summer Sale. You can also tie emails to launches of your latest products or services, or the schedule for your blog or podcast. This will all help you stay focused on specific promotions you want to do throughout the year, and help you repurpose material. Include extracts from your latest blog posts with 'read more ...' links to lead them back on to your site.

Don't build up too many separate email lists, as this can become hard to manage, and you may risk emailing the same people twice. Think instead of segmenting your lists into discrete groups you can send email to – an option that most ESPs have.

Consider getting some help with your email marketing.

Finally, consider getting some help with your email marketing. A virtual assistant or other outsourced professional can help you create email templates, write copy and manage your lists. There are plenty of people who are very experienced with all the major ESPs. See Chapter 16 for advice on finding someone.

Measure your results

One of the many advantages of using a professional email marketing service is that it comes with a wide range of stats and metrics. Most people will open your email – if they're going to – within a few days, so the feedback you get on your campaign (i.e. a single emailing) is fairly quick. Many services will present the information as pie charts or other graphical representations, in a sophisticated amount of detail. Information usually includes:

→ how many people opened your email;

→ how many bounced;

→ how many people classed you as spam;

→ who clicked on to your website from the email;

→ who clicked on specific links within your email;

→ which email clients your subscribers used, e.g. Outlook, Apple Mail, iPhone.

In addition, if you used any unique landing pages and URLs in the links in your emails, you will be able to track these via your webstats. All of this is vital information for following up leads and planning your next campaign.

Email best practice

1 **Warm up your sales** with email signup incentives. Online marketing works well when you give away some content for free with a view to selling something on the same topic later.

2 **Use social networks** to build your email list by promoting your signup giveaways via Twitter, Facebook, LinkedIn, Pinterest, etc.

3 **Ensure you have permission** to include people on your list – use a double opt-in system to be absolutely sure, and include 'unsubscribe' links in every email.

4 **Don't use too many calls to action** in an email – people are more likely to click through if you are simple, clear and focused about what you want them to do.

5 **Split test your subject lines**. Some ESPs, including MailChimp, allow you to split-test your subject lines. That means you can choose different subject fields for the same campaign, and discover which is the most likely to be opened. It will then send some emails with each subject line, see which is the most successful, and send the rest using that subject.

6 **Segment your lists**. Using the Amazon technique of 'if you liked X you might also like Y' to up-sell related products depends on having good data and a sophisticated ESP; but most services allow you to segment your lists according to the preferences people tick when signing up, or groups you add them to. This is easy to manage with MailChimp's Groups function.

7 **Mail your list regularly**. You don't necessarily have to do a weekly or monthly newsletter – you may only email people when you have a new product or special offer. But give list members an idea of what frequency of mailings to expect when they sign up, and mail them regularly enough that they haven't forgotten who you are by the time

your next email arrives and they hit 'mark as spam' because they have forgotten signing up.

8 **Mail when people are most receptive**. Some people think Tuesday is a good day to email because it is the second day of the working week (N.B. this is Mondays in some countries), giving people a day to catch up with important tasks first. But Friday afternoons are popular too, when people are winding down for the weekend. Experiment, and see what works best for your list.

Take action

→ **Choose** an email service provider (ESP).

→ **Build** your email list, making sure to add a signup form to your website.

→ **Plan** your email marketing strategy.

→ **Create** an engaging newsletter that provides value to your customers.

→ **Compose** your first email and measure the results of your campaign.

Get creative

Part Three

Build a blog

How to build trust, reputation and traffic

Chapter Six

According to *The Cluetrain Manifesto* (**www.cluetrain.com**), all markets are conversations. A blog is a great way to start a conversation. It is also your key content tool – and content is the starting point for the value you will add to your marketing activities. Yes, you want to get the word out about your product or service. But social media is also about creating genuinely valuable content that your community will appreciate and want to share. You need to create value – not just ask people to buy from you.

A blog is a great way to start a conversation.

A blog can also be a hub for your social media activity. You can use it to aggregate other media, by including images, video and audio as well as text. You can pull in feeds from other websites, such as your Twitter updates or your Flickr photos. You can create feeds so that people can subscribe to your latest content. And you can encourage sharing with social bookmarking buttons such as 'tweet this', 'like' or 'pin it'.

What is a blog?

A blog, short for 'web log', is a kind of online diary. The author writes entries, or 'posts', which have a date attached, and appear in reverse chronological order – i.e. with the newest entry at the top. Pages can be added as well as posts, via a simple to use content management system. Blogs started as personal journals, but have evolved into something far more powerful, and useful, for business.

There are a number of features of blogs that make them different from an ordinary, static website, including:

1 **Sidebar**. A blog will usually have one or two sidebars – a column or two, usually on the right-hand side of the main part of the screen where your posts appear. This includes extra information and functions.

2 **Categories**. Posts are usually organised into categories to help people browse your content by topic.

3 Tags. These are keywords attached to individual posts, and another way to navigate to the content that your readers are interested in. Many blogs include a 'tag cloud' in the sidebar, which displays the most commonly used tags in different font sizes, with the largest being more popular.

4 Comments. Readers can usually write their own comments on your posts, below what you've written. Comments will usually include the commenter's name, and link back to their own website or blog. This makes blogs a social medium – a forum for discussion and feedback, rather than a broadcast. Comments can be moderated before they go live.

5 RSS feed. People can click on a special link to receive your latest posts as soon as they are published. There are a number of ways they can receive these – such as via an RSS reader or by email. You don't need to worry about how it works, as it's a standard feature that comes with your blog. There are, however, things you can do to manage and promote your feed.

Crucially, a blog is a conversation – not a lecture. Don't just use a blog as a press-release delivery mechanism. It is far more than that. It is a way for you to start a discussion, provide useful information, and connect with your community.

Why blogging works for business

A blog is central to your social media marketing strategy. According to Technorati's 2013 Digital Influence Report, blogs are more influential than social networks in shaping consumers' opinions and purchase decisions. This is unsurprising, since blogging sits squarely in the 'consideration' phase of your sales funnel. Drive traffic to your blog using social networks (the 'awareness' phase) – and use your blog to articulate the benefits of your product or service. But there are other compelling reasons for business blogging. With a blog you can:

1 Build trust with your potential customers and clients. Today trust is in 'people like me' rather than in large organisations. We choose to do business with people we know, like and trust. Your blog is an important way for people to get to know you.

2 **Build an audience**. One reason to start a blog – even before your business is properly up and running – is to start building an audience. Once you have a niche community following, you will be able to find a way to monetise them later – by selling them products and services that fit with their interests.

3 **Increase search engine visibility**. Google and other search engines love blogs. This is because of the way search engine algorithms work. Google believes a site is more valuable if it has regularly updated content and lots of incoming links – which a well-maintained blog has. Also, the more blog posts you write, the more pages you create for Google to index. These things combine to improve your natural search engine rankings.

4 **Drive traffic to your business website**. The search engine friendliness of your blog, plus your promotion of it via social networks, will keep the traffic coming. Ideally, your blog will be on the same domain as your business website and integrated with it – or at least have a prominent link to your business website.

5 **Position yourself as an expert in your field**. By writing insightful, quality posts, and providing useful information to your community, you can become seen as an expert in your niche – whether that is tax law, flower arranging, or coarse fishing.

6 **Reach a wider market**. More people can find you in more ways if you have a blog.

7 **Create value** for your clients or customers by providing useful, valuable, pass-on-able content.

8 **Learn from your customers** by inviting comments and feedback from them. A blog can be useful for doing ad hoc bits of market research, and helps to keep you closer to your market so that you're more aware of what they want.

9 **Create networking opportunities** you never knew existed. It's not just clients and customers who will find you via your blog but also potential business partners. And if you successfully position yourself as an expert, you may even find that speaking, consulting and writing opportunities come your way.

Get Up to Speed with Online Marketing

10 **Build a community**. A blog is a great starting point for building your online community. If you want to go a stage further than standard blogging software will allow, use BuddyPress (from the same people who brought you WordPress) to add social networking features such as profiles and groups to your site.

Blogging in action

How an Alaskan mom reached millions with her do-it-yourself carpentry blog

Ana White (**http://ana-white.com**) lives in Alaska, USA, makes her own furniture and shares hundreds of free plans on her blog. It is this free content, together with prolific blogging and promotion via social networks, that quickly led to her reaching over three million page views per month.

Ana started blogging at the end of 2009 with a free Blogger account and a desire to share her passion for carpentry. In the first year she blogged designs for a wide range of furniture – nearly 400 posts. This relentless blogging alone made the blog hit one million page views in just three months. Then she started using social networks. Ana now has over 180,000 Facebook fans (**www.facebook. com/knockoffwood**), 7,250 Twitter followers (@_anawhite) and a YouTube channel at **www.youtube.com/knockoffwood** with 50 videos, 6,000 subscribers and over a million video views. But Pinterest is the number one referring site, bringing over 6,000 unique visitors per day. She has 30,000 followers at **pinterest. com/knockoffwood**, but relies more on other people pinning her images, and encourages this with the 'Pin it' button on every page of blog. Ana's content is well suited to the visual web – images of inspirational interiors and finished products and educational video tutorials on topics such as sanding are things that people want to consume and share online.

There are now over 500 plans on her blog, all free despite suggestions she starts charging, and most of which now come from reader suggestions. But free content doesn't mean no income. In year two, the blog started earning enough advertising revenue to support her family, and to invest further in the business. Her plans have also appeared in numerous home magazines, and led to a book deal with Random House (*The Handbuilt Home: 34 Simple, Stylish and Budget-Friendly Woodworking Projects for Every Room*). Ana didn't create a blog to market her business: she blogged about her passion – and it became a business.

▶

Get the idea: Start a blog about your interest, expertise or passion – and blog regularly, particularly in your first year. Use visual media – good quality photographs, and video tutorials where appropriate. Give away free content to build up traffic, and market your blog on social networks such as Facebook, Twitter and Pinterest. A business blog can start with a blog rather than a business!

Source: **www.socialmediaexaminer.com/how-alaskan-mom-brings-millions-to-her-carpentry-blog**

Get up to speed with blogging

First of all, familiarise yourself with the blogosphere by reading a few blogs to get the hang of the conventions, possibilities and styles. Subscribe to a few RSS feeds to get the hang of how these work. Then take the plunge! Here are the steps you need to take to get your blog up and running – and other people reading it:

→ Choose a blogging strategy.

→ Create your blog.

→ Set up your RSS feed.

→ Write your first post.

Choose a blogging strategy

In order to get the most from blogging, it pays to spend a bit of time thinking about what you want to achieve. There is more than one way to benefit from the power of the blogosphere – and not all of them involve starting your own blog. You can, of course, use these in combination:

1 **Start your own blog**. This is the obvious strategy. But if you're not quite ready to jump into the blogosphere, but want to benefit from the power of blogging, try the following. These can also be used – and become more effective – when you have your own blog.

2 **Comment on other blogs**. Often overlooked, but an important way of raising your profile. If you read those related blogs you found,

Get Up to Speed with Online Marketing

particularly those with a large readership, and make a considered, thoughtful comment on someone else's post, you've just contributed to a conversation and produced some useful content. Your comment will link back to your own blog or website, and drive traffic to it.

3 **Write guest posts**. Go a stage further than commenting on other people's blogs, and write posts for them. Approach owners of blogs in your field, and ask if you can write a guest posting. If you pitch a post that is interesting and useful to that blog's readership, the blog owner is quite likely to welcome your contribution (it cuts down on his or her workload), and you benefit from exposure to a new audience and a link back to your own blog or website. You can also go a stage further with guest posts and plan a blog tour.

4 **Blogger outreach**. This is an approach famously used in the early days of business blogging by a small South African winery called Stormhoek Wines (**www.stormhoekwines.com**). They gave away bottles of wine to tech bloggers. The bloggers wrote about it, Stormhoek's search engine rankings soared, and the wine became Silicon Valley's tipple of choice. I often recommend that publishers include book bloggers on their review list for the same reason – to engage influencers. It is a strategy that can be applied to most industries. Who are the influencers in your market? What free samples can you send them? What will get people talking?

Frequently asked questions

What is a blog tour?

Popular in the publishing world as a virtual alternative to a physical book tour, a blog tour is an approach that goes one step further than the occasional guest post, compressing several posts on multiple blogs into a short space of time. Some authors do this very successfully, often producing a *lot* of guest posts, such as Seth Godin or Tim Ferriss. This doesn't just apply to books though – it can be a strategy for launching any new product, business or website. And you don't need to go mad and do 60 posts, as they sometimes do: 5–7 posts over a week or so will still have an impact, reach new audiences, and boost your incoming links. It does take some advance planning, and time to write the posts, each of which needs to be tailored to a particular audience. But not all your posts have to be ▶

original articles – you might also do some interviews or Q&As, and some bloggers might want to interview you for their podcast or film a video of you. It all counts towards your blog tour. Don't forget to tell your community about your guest appearances, and link to them from your own blog!

Create your blog

Once you have a blog set up, it is incredibly easy to manage and maintain. The only technical bit is installing the platform in the first place, and this is the part you may need some help with. There are a range of platform options, including Blogger, WordPress and Typepad. I always recommend WordPress to my clients, and use it on all my own blogs: it's free, robust, and endlessly customisable with 'themes' (designs), 'plugins' and 'widgets' (which add extra functionality). Whichever platform you choose, your blogging options really boil down to two choices:

1 **Hosted externally**. If you use **www.blogger.com** or **http://wordpress.com**, you can be up and running in a few minutes. You don't have to worry about installing software, buying web space, or owning a domain name. This is the easy option, and worth considering if you just want to try out blogging to see if it's for you, or if you don't yet have a website or domain name. The downside is that it looks less professional, and you're stuck with a domain name that has 'blogspot' or 'wordpress' in it, such as **http://yourname.blogspot.com** or **http://yourname.wordpress.com**. You can, however, pay to upgrade your WordPress.com account so you can use your own domain name if you wish.

2 **Hosted on your own server**. If you own some web space and have your own domain name (see Chapter 3), you can go to **http://wordpress.org**, download the latest copy of WordPress for free, and install it on your server. This not only looks more professional, but also means:

   – Your blog stays on your own business website – essential for driving web traffic to your business.

   – Your blog is customisable with a wide range of free or commercially available themes. Do a search for 'premium WordPress themes' to find these.

Get Up to Speed with Online Marketing

- You can go a stage further if you wish, and create a bespoke theme – or have one created for you – so that your blog matches your business site and has the exact look, feel and functions you want.

- You have access to a vast number of plugins and widgets to extend the functionality of your blog.

If you start off with wordpress.com, you can always move to a wordpress.org blog later. It is even possible to migrate your content across from wordpress.com to wordpress.org.

The technicalities of WordPress installation are beyond the scope of this book. Some internet service providers (ISPs) allow a one-click install of WordPress from your control panel, which saves the bother of installing it yourself. If you download the software from **http://wordpress. org**, you will need to ensure your server has access to the latest version of the programming language PHP, and that you can connect the software to a MySQL database. If in doubt, ask your ISP.

Think about whether your business blog is to be a discrete section of your website, or if you want your entire website to be a blog. There are advantages to the latter – the main one being that you can also use WordPress as a CMS for your whole site.

Widgets and plugins

WordPress widgets and plugins are additional bits of software that add extra functionality to your blog. They are usually free, and are incredibly useful. Widgets usually appear in your sidebar, and include functions such as your latest comments, latest tweets, or an RSS feed from another blog.

Widgets are for everyone, but plugins are only available to you if you use WordPress.org – the version that you download and host yourself. You can find a comprehensive directory of plugins at **http://wordpress. org/extend/plugins**. Some of the ones I find useful include:

→ **Contact form**. It is important that people can get in touch with you, and there are plenty of plugins out there that will enable you to include a simple contact form to a page on your blog. Some include a CAPTCHA test to reduce spam. Search for 'contact form' in the plugins directory for the most popular ones.

→ **flickrRSS** (**http://eightface.com/wordpress/flickrrss**) displays your Flickr photos on your blog.

→ **Shareaholic email, bookmark, share buttons** (formerly Sexy Bookmarks) (**http://wordpress.org/extend/plugins/shareaholic**) will add social bookmarking buttons such as 'tweet this', 'pin this' and 'share on Facebook' to your blog posts. It also includes buttons to enable your readers to share your content on a wide range of dedicated social bookmarking sites such as Delicious, Digg and StumbleUpon. You can choose from a huge range of buttons in the setting configuration – including 'email this' and 'printer friendly' buttons.

→ **WordPress Audio Player** (**http://wpaudioplayer.com**). With this plugin installed, the link to any MP3 file you include in a post or page will become a Flash media player, so that visitors can play an audio file directly from your blog. This is essential if you are delivering a podcast via your blog (see Chapter 7).

→ **WP-Cumulus** (**www.roytanck.com/2008/03/15/wp-cumulus-released**). There are many plugins to display a 'tag cloud' on your blog – a collection of your keyword tags with the more frequently used tags appearing larger. WP-Cumulus gives you a great, animated version, with your tags spinning in a 3-D globe.

→ **WP Status Notifier** (**http://wordpresssupplies.com/wordpress-plugins/status-notifier**). A simple yet essential plugin if you run a multi-author blog, such as a business blog where a number of your colleagues contribute posts. It simply sends you (or another blog administrator) an email whenever a contributed post is pending your review and approval before it is published. Something you wouldn't otherwise know without this handy plugin.

Set up your RSS feed

One of the things that makes a blog a blog rather than an ordinary, static website is that your readers can subscribe to your latest postings. By clicking on an RSS icon on your blog or in the web address bar, your readers will be taken to a page where they can opt to subscribe, for example by adding your feed to their favourite RSS newsreader.

Why do you want people to subscribe to your RSS feed? Because it means they don't have to keep checking back to your blog to see whether or not you've posted anything new. This is especially important if you don't post very often! If people are subscribed to your feed, they will be alerted whenever you post something new. It can also be useful if you have more than one blog, and want to pull in the RSS feed of one blog into the sidebar of another blog using the built-in WordPress 'RSS Widget' – which you can use with any RSS feed, not just your own.

An RSS feed comes with your blog and works automatically – you don't need to do anything. But you will have many more options if you sign up to FeedBurner (**www.feedburner.com**). Not only do you get access to statistics about how many people subscribe to your feed, which posts are most popular and clicked on, but you also get a wealth of ways to promote your feed.

These include a counter to put on your blog, showing the number of your subscribers; some code to add to your blog to encourage people to subscribe at the end of every post; and, most usefully, an email delivery option (see Chapter 5).

Quick win

Find topics to write about

You have your blog set up. Now, what are you going to write about? If you are a business-to-business (B2B) company, write about developments in the industry you serve. If you are business-to-consumer (B2C) company, what do your customers care about? You can write about your latest company news, products and services – but it's best not to do this too often. Rather than a hard sell, focus instead on useful information that your community will value, and on the topics your target audience wants to read about.

Include plenty of keywords relating to your business, and focus each blog posting on one topic. This will help your search engine rankings. Follow the journalistic principle of starting with the headline, getting the main story into your opening line and then get more detailed.

▶

Include plenty of keywords relating to your business.

To find inspiration for topics to write about, do the following:

→ **Read other blogs** and subscribe to the RSS feeds of ones that are relevant to you and your readers.

→ **Use Google Alerts** for email updates in your area of interest.

→ **Carry a notebook** to jot down ideas as they occur to you.

→ **Be topical**. If you write about, say, the latest Budget statement, or an industry awards dinner you attended, chances are people will be searching for information on that subject.

→ **Solve a problem** for your readers. Any blog post that starts with the words 'How to ...' is usually popular.

→ **Create a list**. Blog posts that start '10 ways to ...' or '7 essential resources for ...' are also popular.

Write your first post

WordPress comes with a powerful built-in text editor. Use it to create new blog posts and pages.

1 Add a title for your blog post. Be aware that this also appears in the permalink (the URL for the individual blog post), so will be the first thing search engines see. Make it relevant to your post and think about keywords.

2 Type your post directly into the text window. If you want to copy and paste from a Word document, you will need to strip out the hidden formatting tags that Word puts into documents, since these will affect the look and format of your post on the blog. To do this, simply click on the **HTML** tab, paste in your text, then switch back to the **Visual** tab to continue editing. You can also use the HTML tab to enter HTML code into your post to give you more control over how it looks.

3 To enter a link, highlight text you want to turn into a link, and click the chain icon. Enter the full URL of the page you want to link to, and a title for the link (optional – this displays when someone hovers over the link). Click update.

Get Up to Speed with Online Marketing

4   To enter an image, click the **Add Media** button just above the text editing window. You can also upload video, audio or other media.

5   To add a video from YouTube, simply copy and paste the embed code supplied by YouTube for the video you want into the HTML window.

6   When you have finished creating your post, add it to a Category. The default category for blog posts is 'Uncategorized'. By putting your blog posts into meaningful categories (you can choose more than one for a single post), you create another way for people to navigate to the content they want.

7   Add tags – keywords that describe what your blog post is about – to further help people to find your post.

8   Once you've finished, you can save your post as a **Draft**, **Preview** how it will look before publishing, or hit the **Publish** button to publish it now. If you want to publish it at some point in the future, just amend the publication date settings. This is useful if you want to write several posts at once, and release them over time – perhaps while you are away.

Manage the workload

In 2008, the *New York Times* identified a phenomenon called 'death by blogging' – exhausted bloggers in digital sweat-shops trying to keep up with the constant demand of the always-on internet economy for fresh news, insight and comment. Some people will tell you that you need to update a blog daily for it to be of any value. How on earth can you keep up? I don't think you need to blog daily – but you do need to maintain the freshness of your content to keep people coming back and your search engine results high. Techniques for making your blogging life easier include:

1   **Schedule time for blogging**. Easier said than done, but you should set aside some time for updating your blog as you would for any other marketing activity – either daily or weekly, depending on how often you plan to write. Consider using an 'editorial calendar' to plan ahead, perhaps with specific topics on specific days of the week.

2 **Batch process your posts**. Write a number of posts in one go, and then schedule them to appear over the next several days or weeks. With WordPress, you can set blog posts to publish on a specific date and time in the future.

3 **Write short posts**. You don't have to write a 2,000-word essay all the time. Break up long posts into shorter entries and publish them over several days. People prefer to read material on the web in bite-sized chunks. You might consider writing one longer post, such as a feature or 'think piece' once a month – and write shorter posts the rest of the time: 350–500 words is fine.

4 **Re-blog other people's posts**. Scan the latest blog posts in your topic using your RSS reader, or search Twitter for interesting, relevant, recent blog posts. You don't always have to write original material yourself. You can post an extract from someone else's blog – making sure you credit the author and link to the full post, of course. You may want to add some words of your own, providing your take on the subject and contextualising it for your readers. This is more useful than just posting links to other blogs.

5 **Save time with Zemanta**. As well as allowing readers to re-blog extracts from the front end, a plugin called Zemanta (**www.zemanta. com**) gives you a bit of editorial help in the back end. As you write, it will automatically suggest links, images and related blog posts that you can add to your post with a single click.

6 **Dictate your posts**. If you really want to speed things up, why not invest in some dictation software? Dragon Dictate is excellent, and available for Mac and PC. Bloggers tend to have a conversational style, after all.

7 **Don't do it all yourself**. Invite other people in your business to write blog posts. This shares the workload and involves and engages them. You may want to invite external people to do an occasional guest blog spot, either by contacting them individually or posting your pitch guidelines on a 'Write for Us' page on your blog. Multi-author blogs are easy to manage with WordPress.

Get Up to Speed with Online Marketing

Measure your results

→ **Webstats**. Look at your website analytics package, such as Google Analytics or Clicky, to analyse how much traffic you're getting and from where. Spot which are the most popular posts, and write more of them.

→ **Feed stats**. Look at your statistics in FeedBurner for a breakdown of who is accessing your RSS feed and how. You may want to include a counter of subscribers on your blog – if your numbers are impressive enough.

→ **Rankings**. Look at where your site ranks by topic on Technorati or blogrankings.com.

→ **Conversational index**. We started this chapter by describing markets as conversations, and blogs as conversation starters. Well, you can measure the level of conversational engagement your blog has. Your conversational index is the number of blog comments divided by the number of blog posts. You're aiming for a number above 1 with this one. The numbers you need to work it out are displayed in your WordPress dashboard. You can also use this measure over a discrete time period, or for a specific category.

Blogging best practice

1 **Post regularly**. Aim to become the 'go to' site for your niche. You don't always have to post original articles – repost extracts from other sources too, so long as you credit the original source and link back.

2 **Plan your posts** in advance with an editorial calendar. Write a batch of posts and schedule them to post on future dates.

3 **Invite others** to contribute – such as your co-workers, but also invite guest posts from your community.

4 **Go on tour**. Consider posting on other blogs and conducting occasional blog tours.

5 **Integrate your social media**. Use your blog as a 'networking hub' to pull in your latest tweets, Flickr photos and other social media; and include links outward to the social networks you use.

6 **Encourage sharing** with social bookmarking buttons such as 'tweet this', 'like' and 'pin it' underneath every post. You can also install the Facebook 'like' button (see **https://developers.facebook.com/docs/reference/plugins/like**).

7 **Market your blog** by automatically posting your blog posts to Twitter and Facebook as you publish them using Twitterfeed.

Take action

→ **Subscribe** to a few blogs in your area to familiarise yourself with the blogosphere.

→ **Create** your blog using WordPress.

→ **Manage** your RSS feed by signing up to FeedBurner.

→ **Find** some topics to write about.

→ **Write** your first post!

Podcast for profit

How to attract an audience of loyal listeners

Chapter Seven

Like radio, podcasting is an intimate medium and a way of building loyal relationships with your audience, as well as conveying useful information and promoting your business without a hard sell. The barriers to producing both audio and video have plummeted in recent years. You no longer need expensive equipment to create these engaging forms of media, a licence to deliver them to your audience, or a vast audience to be profitable. Just a niche topic area, something useful to say, and a willingness to communicate.

What is a podcast?

The term 'podcast' was coined in 2004, by Ben Hammersley in *The Guardian* newspaper. It is a portmanteau of the words 'pod', from iPod, and 'broadcasting'. The word is a little misleading, however, since you don't need an iPod or any MP3 player to listen to podcasts: most people prefer to listen to them from their computers rather than a dedicated media player, according to a 2010 Edison Research survey – though podcast consumption via smartphones is increasing. Despite the radio show format many adopt, it is also not broadcasting either – quite the opposite, in fact, since podcasts reach niche audiences rather than the mass market. The term 'narrowcasting' is more appropriate.

Another thing a podcast is not is a static audio file on a web page. The thing that turns audio files into podcasts is the ability to subscribe to new episodes as they are released, like a magazine. This is achieved by wrapping the audio files in an RSS feed. That sounds frighteningly technical – but isn't. It just means you deliver them on a blog.

When someone subscribes, using a service such as iTunes, new episodes are downloaded when they are ready, and can be listened to from your computer or portable MP3 player. This makes them 'time-shifted media' – unlike a radio show that you have to tune in to at a specific time, a podcast can be listened to whenever and wherever suits the listener. Shows may be regular, e.g. weekly, or you may choose to do a limited run of a few shows leading up to a product launch or event.

Podcasts can also be video files – sometimes called vodcasts. We will concentrate mainly on audio in this chapter, and there is more information on video production in the next chapter.

Podcasts are usually free, but it is also possible to charge for them. However, if you are using a podcast to market your business, it is best to keep it free, and not even charge the price of an email registration. You want to build an audience, not barriers.

Why podcasting works for business

Podcasts have the power to create a bond between you and your customers. Nothing engages your customers like audio and video. Speaking to people directly helps build trust, convey information and articulate what your business has to offer in a far more effective way than reading brochure text on a website.

Nothing engages your customers like audio and video.

A podcast is also another way for people to discover you, since people search on iTunes and other directories for podcasts in their area of interest. By connecting with this community of interest, you can generate customer loyalty – and new business.

Podcasting works for your business by creating a community around it, based on the usefulness of the information you share with potential clients and customers. This also positions you as an expert in your field, and someone who is committed enough to it to put on a show. It is important to use podcasting in this way, rather than as a sales pitch. This is not the place to sell your wares. If you want to do an audio ad, call your local radio station. A podcast, like other forms of social media, should focus on your audience and provide them with something of value. Include a call to action, and the sales will come later.

A podcast, like a blog, is a content tool that becomes more powerful the more content you add. A regular podcast, like a regular blog, builds up a back catalogue of information that people will keep discovering. And since each episode of your podcast will be delivered on a separate page of your blog, along with show notes and possibly even a transcript, there is also plenty of textual content and links for search engines to index.

Podcasting in action

How a pair of property investors topped the iTunes charts by sharing their passion

The Property Podcast is a weekly mix of property news and debate presented by Rob Bence who runs RMP Property (**http://rmpproperty.com**) and Rob Dix who runs Property Geek (**www.propertygeek.net**) – both active property investors and podcast addicts who saw an opportunity to combine their passions.

Soon after its launch in March 2013, the podcast was manually selected for promotion on the iTunes podcast homepage, appeared in the 'New and Noteworthy' list, and regularly beat the BBC's own podcasts to rank number one in the business category. By the end of its second month, it was achieving over 20,000 downloads per month.

The Robs deliberately selected a format that keeps episodes snappy and informal, while sharing valuable information in a medium that previously lacked any kind of property content. It balances entertainment and education, and incorporates plenty of listener interaction. They knew that reviews were important in determining their iTunes rankings, so they made a point of asking for reviews and reading them all out on the show – racking up 65 five-star reviews in their first three months.

The accompanying website, **www.thepropertypodcast.com**, includes transcripts (which help Google rankings), a call to join the show's mailing list, and a way for listeners to leave questions as voicemail messages.

Get the idea: Think about something you're passionate about which is currently poorly served – other people will be hungry for that information too. Decide on a format and a posting schedule, get some attractive artwork, and make the most of the first eight weeks when you're eligible for the 'New and Noteworthy' chart. Above all, never try to sell anything to your audience: interact with them, ask for reviews, and drive them back to your website to get more useful information. The trust they'll build up by spending half an hour a week in your company will generate sales leads without you even having to try.

Get up to speed with podcasting

Podcasting can seem an intimidating social media tool to use, as there is more to it than starting a Facebook group or setting up a blog. But it is really not that scary if you approach it with the same principles as other forms of social media. Think about what valuable, useful content you can provide. Focus on your audience, be relevant, authentic and informal and include a call to action at the end. Don't go for a hard sell – think infotainment rather than infomercial, and leave them wanting more.

The technical aspects are also fairly straightforward if you follow these steps: plan, record, produce, deliver and promote.

→ Plan your podcast – choose a style and format.

→ Record your podcast – choose your equipment.

→ Produce your podcast – editing, post-production and music.

→ Deliver your podcast – via your blog.

→ Promote your podcast – get listed in iTunes.

Plan your podcast

What sort of podcast are you going to produce? What works well in your market? Start with a search in iTunes for keywords in your field, and see what podcasts are available. Subscribe to those that interest you. Note that iTunes has a dedicated section for video podcasts too – have a look there if you're considering video podcasting.

Audio or video?

One of your first decisions is whether to produce an audio or video podcast. This might partly be constrained by the budget available, since audio podcasts are cheaper and quicker to produce. But audio also works well for communicating knowledge. If your content is primarily interviews, you may as well do an audio podcast rather than a video with talking heads. Video podcasts work well when there is a practical, visual, 'how to' element to what you want to communicate. The rest of this chapter will focus on audio podcasts, and there is advice on producing video in the next chapter.

Choosing a style and format

Think about who is going to present your podcast. It is more interesting for the listener if you have a co-host rather than doing it all on your own; and interviewing guests also breaks things up and adds new voices.

Have a listen to some podcasts in your area, or just those whose style you like. You don't have to copy your competition, but if you find a style you like, feel free to adapt it for your niche. Do you want to do a magazine-style show with co-hosts and interviews like *The Guardian*'s Media Talk or *Nature Magazine* podcasts, for example? Listening carefully to well-produced shows like this will give you some clues as to where to play in the intro music, and ideas like highlighting forthcoming interviews with some extracts at the top of the show.

Have a listen to some podcasts in your area.

How long should your podcast be? The received wisdom used to be a maximum of 20–30 minutes for an audio podcast and 5 minutes for a video podcast. I think even shorter than this is better. People have very short attention spans online, and even a 5-minute audio podcast can work, and 1-minute videos are more likely to be watched to the end. However, this isn't right for every audience. Invite feedback on your first few episodes, and your audience will soon tell you if they think it's too long or too short.

Once you start podcasting, don't feel you have to stay on a treadmill of producing half an hour every week forever. You can also do a limited-run podcast of, say, four to eight episodes leading up to a launch or event; or do your podcasts in seasons of six episodes at a time. Survey your audience to find out what works for them – but also plan your podcasting to fit realistically with the demands of your business.

Podcasting styles include round-table discussions, a single interview each episode, and a magazine-style programme with several segments that are common to every show. Plan your format as you might for a radio or TV programme. For example:

Intro	Industry news	Feature/ Interview	Tips/How-to feature	Ending

Then sketch out a grid to plan your shows in advance. You can record some items in advance – just keep a note on your grid of which things are yet to be recorded. Think about your timings at this stage too. For example:

Item	Duration	Ep1	Ep2	Ep3
Intro	00:30	Intro	Intro	Intro
News	04:30	Item name	Item name	Item name
Interview	06:00	Item name	Item name	Item name
Tips	03:30	Item name	Item name	Item name
Ending	00:30	Music	Music	Music
TOTAL	15:00			
			Recorded	To be recorded

Record your podcast

You don't need to hire a recording studio to capture good quality audio. The quality of your microphones is the most important factor.

Hardware

Clip-on tie microphones offer good quality, especially for round-table discussions. For recording yourself directly on to your computer, use a microphone that plugs into your computer's USB port rather than one with a standard jack – the quality is much better. You can pick up a good USB microphone, such as the Samson C01U USB Studio Condenser Microphone, for about $125/£80.

A portable digital recorder is useful for recording interviews on the move. The Zoom H2 Handy Recorder (about $190/£120) is popular with many podcasters.

Interviews

Interviews are a great way of providing useful information and new perspectives for your listeners. You can do interviews in person or using free internet telephony such as Skype (**www.skype.com**) with a recording application called Pamela (**www.pamela.biz**).

Give your guests a fighting chance by giving them some idea of what you want to ask them first – a list of questions or topics in advance. That doesn't mean that you should script your podcast, or that you can't explore other questions and topics that arise during the conversation – it just primes your guest on what to expect, and helps them prepare their thoughts. It will produce a more useful interview from a more confident guest.

Don't record anyone without their permission.

It can be a good idea to have your guests sign an interview release – though, in practice, podcasting is a fairly informal medium and this is rarely done. Bear in mind general journalistic guidelines and ethics when interviewing. See the UK Press Complaints Commission's 'Editors' Code of Practice' at **www.pcc.org.uk/cop/practice.html** for an example of this. Above all, don't record anyone without their permission.

Produce your podcast

Once you have recorded your audio content, in the form of interviews and discussion, it's time for post-production. This means editing out pauses and mistakes (don't over edit, though), piecing together your different items and interviews, adding any music and sound effects, and exporting the whole thing as an MP3 file.

Audio editing software

To edit your audio, use some great free software called Audacity for the PC or Mac (**http://audacity.sourceforge.net**). Mac users can also use GarageBand (**www.apple.com/ilife/garageband**). Audacity is very powerful and can be used to work on multiple, overlapping tracks on a single timeline – such as your introduction, interviews and music – and then to combine them into a single file.

Output

Output your finished work as an MP3 file. You can do this with Audacity, but you will need to install something called a LAME MP3 Encoder first. This is free, and instructions are supplied by Audacity. Be sure to add ID3 tags to your MP3 file too – these specify information that is contained within your audio file such as genre, author and title. Do a search for 'ID3 tag editor' to find free software you can use to do this.

Frequently asked questions

Where can I find music to use in my podcast?

You need to make sure you have permission to use any music you need. Music Alley (**www.musicalley.com**) is a good place to find licensed music. However, for an opening theme tune, I recommend AKM Music (**www.akmmusic.co.uk**) – a great source of affordable, licensed music used by big brands and broadcasters such as the BBC. With a large database of music categorised by style, you're sure to find something appropriate that fits your 'audio branding'. You may also find some music that you can download and use with permission at SoundCloud (**http://soundcloud. com**). For sound effects, try Soundsnap (**www.soundsnap.com**), a community of audio producers creating and uploading audio loops and sound effects.

Deliver your podcast

Host your audio files

Now that you've created your MP3 audio file, it's time to share it with the world! The first step is to host it on a website. You have two options here:

1 A podcast hosting service – there are various services that will host your audio or video podcast for you, such as jellycast.com and podbean.com.

2 Your regular web hosting service – just upload your audio files to your normal web server in a separate folder called 'podcasts'.

Create a blog or a blog category

Next, you need to deliver your audio files on a blog. Create a new blog post for each podcast episode, either on a blog dedicated to your podcast, or on your business blog with a 'podcast' category. Include a title and show notes. These should comprise a short paragraph explaining what is on the episode, a list of topics or items covered with timings, and links to any websites mentioned.

Don't forget to create a link to the MP3 audio file you uploaded, and make sure it can be played on the page. Use a WordPress plugin (such as WordPress Audio Player – **http://wpaudioplayer.com**) that automatically turns links to audio files into a media player, so that people can listen to your podcast directly from your website without having to download it first. Some WordPress themes come with this function built in.

Create an RSS feed in FeedBurner

Whether your podcast is delivered on a dedicated blog or a discrete category of your main blog, an RSS feed will be created for it. However, don't use this as the main feed for your podcast, such as the one you submit to iTunes. Create a new feed in FeedBurner first. This is as simple as it is to create a FeedBurner feed for your blog – just make sure you check the 'I am a podcaster' box when you set up your feed in order to access the additional options you need for a podcast feed.

Select the 'include iTunes podcasting elements' in FeedBurner and add the data iTunes requires there. Additional items you need to include in your RSS feed, to provide the data that iTunes and other directories require, include a category, subcategory, description and keywords for your podcast. You also need a 'podcover' – a 300 × 300 pixel .jpg graphic that is the equivalent to a record sleeve or book jacket for your podcast. Enter a weblink for this in the image field. If you use the PodPress plugin in WordPress, this data will already be included in your feed, and you won't need to enter it into FeedBurner.

FeedBurner will provide you with the same range of statistics and promotional tools, including subscription by email, as you get for a standard blog feed.

Quick win

Create an instant podcast with Audioboo

Audioboo (**http://audioboo.fm**) is a very easy way to create audio files from your iPhone or computer, and share them with your community. You can record audio clips of up to 3 minutes with a free account, and up to 30 minutes with a Plus account (£60/year or £6.99/month).

Get Up to Speed with Online Marketing

You can automatically tweet your 'boos' and share them on Facebook. What's more, people can subscribe to your boos in iTunes, making it an easy way to create an instant, ad hoc podcast without worrying about blogs, RSS feeds or recording equipment.

→ Create an account at **http://audioboo.fm**.

→ Upload a profile image, add a brief biography, and make sure to include your web address.

→ Before you start booing, do a keyword search to find some boos in your area of interest, to get a feel for what people are doing, and relevant people to follow.

→ If you have an iPhone, download the free iPhone app. It is also possible to record boos and upload them from your computer. But booing works best on the move.

→ Record your first boo. This doesn't have to be an interview – you can just introduce yourself and your new Audioboo account and say what you'll be using it for. It doesn't have to be slick or professional. The beauty of Audioboo is its brevity and immediacy.

→ Upload your boo along with a photo, which you can take with your iPhone if you are using the app. This might be of the person you were speaking to. Include a title for your boo, and tag it with some keywords to help people find it.

→ Audioboo then creates a page for your boo, with a media player to play back your audio, the photo you uploaded, and a map showing where you recorded it – since your iPhone knows where you are! You can opt out of the map if you want, and photos are optional too – but both add useful context.

→ Your page also includes social bookmarking buttons to 'tweet', 'like' and '+1' your boo (i.e. share it on Twitter, Facebook or Google+), and a link to some embed code so that other people can embed your audio on their own blog or web page. You can also use this on your own site to raise awareness of your boos; and be sure to include a link on your website. Your Audioboo profile page also includes buttons to subscribe to all of your boos by RSS or via iTunes.

▶

> → Gain greater exposure for your boos by automatically tweeting them and posting them to Facebook, among other social sites available. This has the added benefit of contributing useful content to those accounts.
>
> → Use Audioboo whenever you have the chance to speak with an expert in your field at a conference or trade fair. Many people use Audioboo to have a quick chat with conference speakers during breaks, drinks, or when they visit an exhibition stand. You may also want to share the logins with any colleagues who have an iPhone.

Promote your podcast

Get listed in iTunes

iTunes is the Google of podcast directories – you absolutely must get it listed here. Others include Podbean.com, Podcast Alley, PodcastDirectory.com, Podcast Pickle, blubrry and Odeo – but the vast majority of people will go straight to iTunes.

1 Open the iTunes program. You can download this for free from **www.apple.com/itunes** if you don't have it.

2 Sign in to the iTunes Store. You'll need to create an account if you don't already have one.

3 Click on the 'Podcasts' section in the top navigation.

4 Click 'Submit a Podcast' in the right-hand menu.

5 Enter in your podcast feed URL. Make sure this is the one you created in FeedBurner rather than your original feed address from your blog, so that FeedBurner can track your stats.

6 Confirm the on-screen details, and click 'Submit'. You'll receive an email once your podcast has been accepted by iTunes. This typically takes about a week.

Promote your podcast online

Include a prominent link to your podcast on your own website, including buttons to subscribe in iTunes and by RSS. You might also consider a media player in your sidebar that plays your latest episode.

Include a prominent link to your podcast on your own website.

Make sure your show notes for each episode include plenty of keywords, and links to any websites you mention. You might even consider including a full transcript for each episode. This has two benefits: it makes your podcast more accessible; and it creates a large amount of text on your blog that can be indexed by search engines, making you more findable.

Every time you release a new episode, tell your email list, tweet about it and mention it on Facebook, LinkedIn, Google+ or whichever social networks you use.

Create community

Just as people can leave text comments on your blog, invite them to submit audio comments on your podcast. Set up a Skype answering service, or use a blog plugin such as SpeakPipe (**http://wordpress.org/ extend/plugins/speakpipe-voicemail-for-websites**) to create a widget that captures audio or video comments. Not everyone is comfortable 'phoning in' comments, so invite comments by email, Twitter, Facebook, etc., or by commenting on the blog post for your podcast episode. You might even put a call out on Twitter for people to record their own Audioboos for potential inclusion on your next podcast. Ask them to let you know when they've done this, or to add a hashtag specific to your podcast so you can find their comments. Make sure that people are clear about how their comments will be used.

Encourage your community to review your podcast on iTunes. A podcast with reviews is more likely to be subscribed to by new listeners.

Get interviewed on other podcasts

This is the podcasting equivalent of a guest posting on someone else's blog, and can form part of your blog tour. Search iTunes for relevant podcasts, then approach the host by email.

Measure your success

Your customer ratings and reviews on iTunes will give you a sense of how well received your podcast is, along with feedback on your blog and audio comments. But there are other quantitative statistics you can use too:

→ Your FeedBurner statistics will tell you how many subscribers you have.

→ Your webstats will tell you how many times your audio files have been downloaded.

→ If you use a podcast hosting service, it should provide these stats.

→ If you use unique landing pages – a web address that is only mentioned once on a specific podcast – you can measure how many people have taken action as a result of listening to your show and visited your website.

Podcasting best practice

1 **Keep it relevant, authentic and informal**. There's nothing worse than a stilted, scripted podcast! Know your audience and what they want – make it entertaining, insightful and useful to them.

2 **Keep it brief**. You don't have to do a weekly half-hour show. Try bite-sized five to ten minute shows, and see how your audience reacts. Consider doing a limited run podcast, at least at first, to test the response you get.

3 **Don't do a hard sell**. The focus should be on the information, not what you're selling.

4 **Include a call to action**. Include only one call to action, to avoid confusing people – and put it at the end of your podcast so that people have the chance to consume your content first (another reason to keep it brief!).

5 **Use your blog**. The easiest way to deliver a podcast is via a separate category on your existing blog. Upload an audio file for a single episode to a single blog post, include 'show notes', and use FeedBurner to create the RSS feed to deliver your podcast.

Take action

→ **Listen** to a few podcasts in your field, to research your market.

→ **Plan** your podcast style and format.

→ **Record** your first podcast – interview an expert in your field.

→ **Produce** your first podcast – familiarise yourself with Audacity.

→ **Deliver** your podcast using a blog and FeedBurner.

→ **List** your podcast in iTunes.

→ **Promote** your podcast on your website, with email and via your social networks.

Lights, camera, action!

How to produce online video on a budget

Chapter Eight

The wide take-up of broadband has made watching video online an integral part of many people's internet browsing experience. TV is becoming integrated with the internet as people increasingly watch film and TV shows online. You no longer need a vast budget and a film crew to produce compelling video. The barriers to entry to using this medium have dropped as the cost of equipment and software has decreased, and it is easier than ever to create your own video and upload it to free video sharing sites such as YouTube. As a business, you can use this as a powerful means of communicating directly with your clients and customers.

You no longer need a vast budget and a film crew to produce compelling video.

What is online video?

In 2013 YouTube achieved figures of one billion unique visitors and four billion hours of video watched per month. It is the third most popular site in the world, according to Alexa, behind only Google (which owns it) and Facebook.

The fact that Google owns it also now means that it is nicely integrated with Google+ – there are '+1' social sharing buttons next to every video, you can watch a video with friends using a Google+ hangout, and you have a YouTube tab on your Google+ profile that shows videos you have uploaded. But you can easily share videos with – and play them within – many other social networks, including Facebook, Twitter and Pinterest.

Other video sharing sites are available, notably Vimeo (**www.vimeo. com**), but the sheer size and reach of YouTube makes this an important place to be if you want to engage your customers with video.

While putting a static piece of video on your website will engage your visitors and help your search engine results, it is not social media. If you upload your video to a video sharing site and then embed it back on your site (simple to do with the code supplied), it provides another way for people to find and interact with you. They can comment on your video, add it to their 'favourites' and embed it in their own websites or blogs.

It is also possible to record and upload short video clips from your smartphone, for example using Vine (6-second video loops you share on Twitter) or Instagram (up to 15 seconds). While this can be useful for short interviews, announcements or updates, we will focus on more substantial videos in this chapter, which you will share on YouTube or Vimeo.

Why online video works for business

Video works because it offers you a chance to show your wares to prospective customers or clients – whether you're a plumber, a business coach or a travel agent. It works particularly well where there is a visual element to your business – such as video tours of your properties if you are a real estate agent; or if you need to educate your market in some way – such as in bicycle maintenance if you sell bikes. But most businesses can find a way to use video successfully. In addition, video will allow you to do the following:

→ Boost your search engine rankings if you include it on your website. Search engines like websites with rich media content, and Google features YouTube videos prominently in its Search Engine Results pages.

→ Provide another way for people to find you. YouTube describes itself as the second biggest search engine.

→ Enhance your brand recognition.

→ Encourage people to pass on your marketing message. If your video contains information of interest to a niche audience, bloggers writing about your subject area can embed your videos into their posts.

→ Put a human face on your business.

→ Educate your market, especially if your product or service is complicated to explain.

→ Reduce the amount of time you spend on customer support and queries, by providing all the instruction your customers need in video tutorials. Useful if you sell software or other technical products, for example.

→ Screen out the wrong type of client for your business. Sometimes, if people don't understand your product or service, you can waste time on a prospective client before either of you realise that what he or she needs and what you can offer don't match. Video is one of the clearest ways to articulate exactly what it is that you do.

Online video in action

How an Australian shoe retailer tripled sales with a video giveaway

Shoes of Prey (**www.shoesofprey.com**) is an Australian online shoe store that enables visitors to design their own bespoke shoes, which are hand-made and shipped all over the world. They boosted sales by using video – but not one they created themselves: by engaging with a YouTube phenomenon called Blair Fowler (also know as juicystar07). Her YouTube channel at **www.youtube.com/user/ juicystar07** has over 230 million video views with 1.3 million subscribers tuning in to her fashion and make-up tips for teenage girls. Shoes of Prey arranged a giveaway with Fowler – a competition for her followers, with a pair of shoes as the prize. She announced this to her viewers with a YouTube video (**www.youtube.com/ watch?v=YQ-FrWOKraM**).

In the week it went live, Fowler's giveaway video was the fifth most viewed video on YouTube, and the second most discussed video worldwide. It had over 450,000 views and more than 90,000 comments – each of which was a potential customer who had visited **www.shoesofprey.com**, designed a pair of shoes, then written a description of those shoes and what event they would wear it to.

Shoes of Prey gained more web traffic in two days than in the company's entire previous history. Design-your-own-shoe entrepreneur Michael Fox said on his blog: 'We've now had over 700,000 visits to the Shoes of Prey website, and 500,000 of those came last week!' In addition to blogging about their experience, they went to work on capitalising on the success of the video by enhancing their other social media. This included monitoring mentions on Twitter and making it easy to share designs on Facebook, resulting in converting that extra traffic into sales and a permanent 300 per cent uplift in sales.

Get the idea: Creating your own video can be time consuming and technical. Are there influencers already reaching your target market with their YouTube channels or video blogs? Think about how you can engage them. This doesn't have to be with a giveaway – you could also offer to be interviewed as an expert in your field as a way of promoting yourself and providing value to the video blogger's community. Social media marketing can be about getting people to talk about your stuff – finding the influencers in your market, making it easy for them to talk about your products, and giving them an incentive to do so.

Get up to speed with online video

How you go about creating your video content depends on how ambitious you want to be, the production values you deem necessary, the time you have available, your level of technical skill and what sort of video you want to produce. You don't need a film school degree to get started with your own videos. For a small investment you can buy a cheap camera and upload clips direct to YouTube. In this section, we shall look at how to:

→ Decide what to produce.

→ Choose your equipment.

→ Film a studio-based interview.

→ Edit and output your video.

→ Share your video.

Decide what to produce

Whether you do it yourself or hire a video production company, the first step is to decide exactly what sort of video you want to produce. As with any form of social media marketing, the content you produce must be guided by what your community of interest will find of value. This can be quite specific and niche – in fact it's better if it is. You're not competing with the high-end TV ads of big brand advertising. Often a talking head is just fine.

Decide exactly what sort of video you want to produce.

Lord Reith's mission statement for the British Broadcasting Corporation in 1927 – to inform, educate and entertain – is a good guiding principle for producing video to support your business. You do, of course, have a fourth goal – to sell – but if you think 'infotainment' rather than 'sales pitch', your video will be more engaging, more widely viewed and more likely to be passed on.

Consider your reasons for wanting to use video. What are your goals? They might include to generate sales, drive traffic to your website, raise brand awareness or reduce customer support costs. Here are some options to consider:

→ A **welcome message** on your website shows a human face behind the business.

→ **Client testimonials** are more engaging and convincing if presented as a compilation of short video interviews rather than a few lines of text.

→ **Interviews**, discussions or pieces to camera, filmed in 'studio' conditions with professional lighting present a professional image, and can convey useful information about your product, service, or topic.

→ **Infomercials** are more interesting than straight video ads. If you can get across some useful information that also mentions your product or service, it's much more likely to be viewed and shared.

→ **Product demonstrations** work when your product needs explanation or instructions, and can cut down on customer support time. Do you run a garden centre? How about a video showing us how to prune the roses you sell? You will find plenty of examples of exactly that on YouTube.

→ **Training videos** are a softer sell, yet by providing useful information in your area of expertise (but with the web address of your business at the end), they will draw people on to your site. Evans Cycles has a series of around 50 'how-to' bike maintenance videos at **www.youtube.com/user/evanscycles**, for example. If you have an area of expertise, why not show us what you can do?

Whichever approach you take, keep it short! Even a three-minute video strains attention spans online. Some of the most successful videos are 60–90 seconds long. You want people to stay watching long enough to get to your 'call to action' at the end.

Choose your equipment

Most forms of online marketing are free. However, like podcasting, in order to create video content, you will need to spend a bit of cash. The good news is that you don't necessarily need to spend a fortune. The minimum hardware you will require is a video camera and a computer. You will also need some video editing software.

Camera

You don't need high-end professional gear. There are plenty of hand-held pocket cameras available, which are high enough quality for most purposes. And great when you're out and about and want to grab a quick interview with someone. I'm currently using the Kodak PlaySport Zx5, which films in HD, is shockproof and waterproof, and will share your videos directly to your social networks when you plug it into your computer (if you want). Do a search for 'pocket camcorders' to find a list of ones that are currently popular. You shouldn't need to pay more than around $150/£100.

The downside of many handheld cameras is that the audio from the built-in microphone will never be quite as good as a soundtrack recorded using external microphones. So be sure to get close to your subject to capture the best audio possible. Whichever camera you choose, make sure you have a data card with enough capacity to record the video you need. I use a 32GB high-speed card. You can also record and upload video from many smartphones. This is useful for capturing current events – a growing trend as video and audio increasingly become part of the real-time web.

If you want something more substantial – perhaps if you are doing a lot of studio-based interviews – you don't need a professional level video camera or something that will produce broadcast standard video (and, if you do, hire someone to do this for you). Go for a consumer video camera, but as high-end as you can afford; or a good digital SLR camera with the option to record video. Key things to look out for include:

→ The ability to attach external microphones. Don't rely on the built-in microphone on your camera. The end result may be too quiet, and sound a bit cheap. Use an external microphone, such as a shotgun microphone attached to the top of your camera or clip-on tie microphones. Alternatively, you can record a separate soundtrack using the equipment discussed in the podcasting chapter and combine it with your video footage in the edit.

→ Manual settings, such as the ability to set the 'white balance' and use manual focus.

→ A camera that records in high definition is useful, as video standards improve online. This is increasingly the norm for most digital video cameras.

Lights

If microphones are essential to the quality of your podcast, lighting is essential for video. If you're doing quick and informal clips, you may be able to get away with your pocket camera and use the available light. For something more professional, particularly for studio-based interviews and pieces to camera, consider some 'continuous lighting'. This means studio lights that stay on all the time, as opposed to flash lighting used in still photography. You will need a minimum of two lights – and ideally three.

Lighting is essential for video.

For a professional studio look, use three-point lighting, arranged as shown in Figure 8.1. Your main or 'key' light is the primary lighting source for your subject. The second light is to fill in the shadows, and should be used with a diffuser. The third light is above and slightly behind your subject's head, and separates him or her from the background with a halo of light. You will see this technique used on any TV show with talking-head punditry – look out for it.

Film a studio-based interview

A studio-based interview is the best way to have full control over the sound and lighting conditions, and create a professional-looking piece.

FIGURE 8.1 Three-point lighting

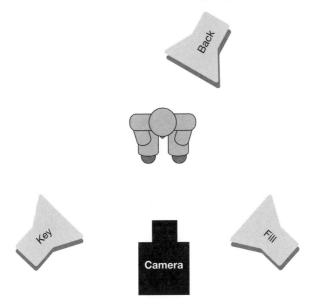

When I say 'studio', I don't mean you have to hire a TV studio. Any quiet room where you won't be disturbed will do – your office, a room you hire, even a location such as a trendy bar that you can hire out for a few hours. Your location should suit the tone of your video.

Your location should suit the tone of your video.

Lights

Set up your three-point lighting as described above. If there are windows, keep the blinds or curtains open, unless bright sunlight is interfering with your shot. If there are lights in the room, switch them all on. Use all available light as well as your studio lighting.

Camera

Use a tripod to steady your camera. Set the focus manually by zooming right in on your subject's nose, adjusting the focus until it's sharp, then zooming back out again. With all your lights on, set the 'white balance' by asking your subject to hold a piece of white paper in front of their face. Zoom in until this fills the screen. Set the white balance according to your camera's instructions, and zoom out again. This removes any 'colour cast' from artificial lighting, and ensures the colours in your finished video will be correct.

Action!

If you are interviewing someone – such as a client, a colleague or an expert in a particular field – you can either prime them with a few questions to respond to beforehand; or ask them questions from behind the camera (you can edit these out later). Make sure you gather all the video material you will need to edit from. Depending on how scripted the piece is, how fluent the speaker is, and how many takes you need, I would suggest you need up to half an hour of footage to create a three to five minute final piece.

The rule of thirds

Photographers often use the 'rule of thirds' to compose shots. This works well for filming interviews too. It just looks odd if the subject is in the middle of the screen. Instead, imagine the screen is divided into nine equally sized segments – three across and three down.

FIGURE 8.2 The rule of thirds.

SEE MY VIDEO INTERVIEW BY ADAM WESTBROOK AT VIMEO.COM/17914551

Get Up to Speed with Online Marketing

Position your subject so that they're caught in the top-left or top-right crosshairs of these imaginary lines. Right between the eyes!

Styles can be:

→ **A piece direct to camera** – the subject looks directly at the camera and says their piece. This isn't really an interview (though there might be someone prompting with questions from behind the camera), but it might be appropriate for filming a welcome message for your website.

→ **Invisible interviewer** – an interviewer, the director or camera operator asks questions from behind and to one side of the camera. The subject looks at the person asking the questions, NEVER at the camera. This creates a more professional image, and is the style you will see most commonly on documentaries and 'talking heads' shows. This is a style that works well for business videos because it looks more journalistic – like you are sharing useful information or insights. If you do this direct to camera it looks 'pitchy' – like you are selling something.

→ **Visible interviewer** – a more documentary style where the interviewer asks the subject questions on camera.

→ **Discussion** – where there are two or three subjects having a discussion about a set topic. It is best if this is unscripted, but essential that the participants are clear about the topics to be covered, and a 'pre-discussion' is useful before the camera rolls (though you may film this too as there could be usable footage). Subjects should generally not look at the camera, though sometimes treating the camera as an extra person in the conversation can work.

Frequently asked questions

What are 'noddies'?

Where you have more than one person on camera, it is more interesting to show reaction shots and use close-ups of individuals speaking than a continuous mid-shot of everyone. You can do this with a single camera by filming 'noddies' – reaction shots of the interviewer or other participants in a discussion nodding ▶

or listening intently to what others are saying. These can be filmed after the discussion. The other reason for using noddies and other camera angles is that they can be used to cover up edits. You will probably want to use only parts of the footage you gather, and don't want the edits to jump and jar. Cut away to a reaction shot or close-up to cover up those jumps. The other way to cover edits is with 'B-roll'. This was traditionally additional footage shot by an extra, 'B' camera, such as establishing shots of the location of the shoot. You can film all of this with the same camera of course – or even buy stock video footage from iStockphoto (**www.istockphoto.com**) or Pond5 (**www.pond5.com**).

Edit and output your video

A full explanation of video editing is beyond the scope of this book. The most important advice is that you should always use timeline-based video editing software. This means that you can add your soundtrack, music, video footage, images, titles, captions, effects and transitions to a single timeline and have a much greater degree of control. I recommend Adobe Premiere Elements, which is now available for both Mac and PC and is less than $150/£100. This is a cut-down version of the full software, but perfectly fine for your needs. You are not making a feature film, after all.

Premiere Elements has two main editing views: Sceneline and Timeline. Timeline is what you will use most of the time, but you will need to use Sceneline to add 'transitions' (any fades and dissolves between clips). In the past, we always used to output a soundtrack first and then edit video clips to it. There is no need for this laborious approach now. If you recorded a separate soundtrack, just make sure you link it to your video *before* you start. In Premiere Elements, the video you import will be linked to its own source soundtrack. If you are using a separately recorded soundtrack instead, you can split these, delete the audio, import your own audio and link it back to the video. Then you're ready to go with editing your clips, adding noddies, cutaways and B-roll to cover your edits.

You can also add images to your video, and should start and end with a 'slate' screen – a static image that might include a title, your company logo or a URL. The final screen should normally be your web address, since this will be the call to action – to visit your website.

Once you've finished editing your video, you need to 'encode' it in a standard video format. You will find a number of preset options for this in your video editing software.

Share your video

Regularly sharing video will help keep your audiences engaged. Other video sharing sites are available, but I think the choice for small business owners really boils down to a straight one between YouTube or Vimeo. Both provide 'embed' code so that you can put videos back on your own blog or website, and allow others to do the same. And don't forget to promote your video on your social networks!

YouTube (**www.youtube.com**)
Unique monthly visitors: 1 billion
Alexa rank: 3
YouTube's popularity means it is still most likely to be your first port of call. Because of the sheer volume of material on YouTube, it is the

first place most people will go to to search for a video, and videos also show up prominently in Google search results. A wide range of quality levels, resolutions and video formats can be used. You can upload videos of up to 10 minutes in length – but shorter is better.

YouTube's popularity means it is still most likely to be your first port of call.

Vimeo (www.vimeo.com)

Unique monthly visitors: 70 million
Alexa rank: 132
Vimeo prides itself on having the highest-quality video on the internet and is positioned more as a community of creative video producers and indie filmmakers. Vimeo was the first video sharing site to support HD. Because it insists users upload material they have produced themselves (rather than the endless clips of TV shows you will find on YouTube), the quality also comes across in the original content.

Social networks

A service called Vine, introduced in January 2013, allows Twitter users to record and tweet 6-second looping videos. In June 2013, photo sharing site Instagram introduced video, enabling users to upload up to 15 seconds of material. These methods of uploading brief clips on the go and sharing them with your networks help with engagement. But the more substantial videos you produce to upload to YouTube or Vimeo should also be promoted via your social networks.

Facebook also allows you to upload videos – but it makes more sense to upload videos to YouTube or Vimeo and then share them on Facebook if you want to, since you can also use them elsewhere.

You can share these videos on your Facebook profile and pages, Twitter, Google+ and even Pinterest, and your fans and followers can play your video directly within the social network without having to leave the site. This means it is more important than ever to include a 'call to action' (usually a web address) at the end of your video, since many people will only see it in isolation on a social networking site rather than on your YouTube channel with a link in the notes, or on your website with an email signup box underneath it.

Manage the workload

The work involved in creating online video is in producing it in the first place, rather than the maintenance. It may be something you do relatively infrequently compared with, say, blogging. But you should still check in to your YouTube channel periodically to 'favourite' a few videos, and respond to friend requests and comments. Ways to maximise your effectiveness while minimising the work include:

→ Whenever you film interviews, do several in one day if you can, so that you only have to set up and break down your equipment once. This is often the most time-consuming part, after editing.

→ Use a pocket camcorder for quick interviews on the move. If you use your iPhone to shoot video, try out Vine or Instagram to see how creative you can be within the time constraint of 6 or 15 seconds!

→ Create a video using Camtasia Studio or from a collection of still images with a voiceover.

→ Sign up to YouTube email notifications so that you know when someone comments on your video without having to monitor the site.

→ Click on **Connected accounts** in your YouTube Account Settings. Connect to your Google+, Facebook and/or Twitter accounts, and decide what you want to share. This can include notifying people when you upload or simply 'like' a video.

→ Record a video via Google+ using a Hangout. Check **Enable hangouts on Air** before you start and your Hangout will be recorded and automatically saved to your YouTube account.

→ Create a YouTube channel even if you don't plan to create and upload videos yet. You can benefit from YouTube and create a useful channel without the workload if you 'favourite' a selection of videos you think your community will find useful.

Measure your results

There are various measures of success that you can use, depending on how you set up your URLs and what your goals are. And YouTube enables you to go beyond simply the number of views with its own metrics. Click on the bar chart 'Statistics' icon beneath any video. You can see these for any video, unless the owner has disabled them – not just your own. Metrics shown include:

→ **Views** – number of views shown on a graph, over time.

→ **Key discovery events** – such as when the video was first searched for on YouTube or embedded on a specific site.

→ **Engagement** – number of comments, favourites, likes and dislikes, expressed as numbers and small graphs.

→ **Audience** – top demographics, such as 'Female, 35-44 years'.

That will tell you something about who your videos are popular with and where. But you can go a stage further and measure who *took action* as a result of watching your video. By using a unique URL – a web address that is only ever mentioned on a specific video – you will be able to tell how many people have not only watched your video but also responded to your call to action. A unique URL can refer on to wherever you actually want the viewer to land, but you will be able to see from your webstats how many people took this journey. Use a unique URL in the video itself, such as in a caption or on the end slate screen, so that it is visible when the video is embedded in another site or watched from within Facebook, Twitter, Pinterest and other social sites.

If you don't want to use unique URLs or just want a more general idea of the effectiveness of your videos in driving traffic to your site, you can still discover a lot from your web analytics. Measure your traffic before and after you use video, and look at where the traffic is coming from.

If one of your goals is to reduce customer support queries, take a measure of the number of these before and after you use videos offering product demos or other customer support.

If your goal is raising brand awareness, you will need to use slightly more traditional means to discover your effectiveness, and conduct market research into your brand perception, including questions about where people first heard about you.

Video best practice

1 **Think about your audience**. Think 'infotainment' rather than advertising – make sure your content is engaging and relevant to the people you are trying to reach.

2 **Educate your market**. People frequently search YouTube for video tutorials. If your business has a practical element, show them how to do something related to your brand.

3 **Plan in advance**. Scripting and storyboarding might not be necessary, but have a very clear idea of what you want the finished product to look like, as this will help you gather all the footage you need before you start editing.

4 **Use good quality equipment**. Use three-point lighting where possible for studio interviews, and use good quality clip-on microphones. Your camera doesn't need to be too high-end so long as you have good sound and lighting.

5 **Use the rule of thirds** to compose your shot when doing interviews.

6 **Re-record parts of your interview** for 'noddies' and shoot B-roll footage or acquire stock footage from **iStockphoto.com**.

7 **Embed your videos** on your site, having uploaded them to YouTube or Vimeo.

8 **Use unique web addresses** as calls to action in your videos so that you can measure your results.

Take action

→ **Create** a YouTube channel for your business.

→ **Connect** to your Facebook, Twitter and Google+ accounts.

→ **Define** your business goals and choose a style of online video.

→ **Choose** your equipment.

→ **Film** an interview.

→ **Edit**, output and share your first video.

Show, don't tell

How to showcase your business on photo sharing sites

They say a picture paints a thousand words, and that is truer than ever on the internet. We don't have the time or attention span to read a lot of text – show us an image instead. 'Show, don't tell' is an adage familiar to any film student. Don't have one of your characters *tell* us the story with a lot of plot exposition when you could *show* it on screen. The same applies to telling your business story. Yes, you can write an essay on your 'About Us' page – and that will help search engine results and keen readers – but if you want to grab attention quickly, include images too. Better still is to share your images on sites such as Instagram and Flickr as well, to reach a wider audience, engage them on the sites they are using, and draw them onto your own website.

What is photo sharing?

Photo sharing is the uploading and sharing of your images on a third-party website. Most are free, at least to use a basic account with limited storage space. Most allow members to comment on each other's images, and to 'tag' their images with keywords to aid searching. Images can often be rated and favourited, and members normally have a profile page with more information about them. This is usually the one place where you are allowed to mention your business, and link to it.

Various photo sharing sites exist, including Instagram, Flickr, Blipfoto, Picassa and Snapfish. Not all of these are suited to business use. Some are better for image hosting or serious photography hobbyists. The two biggest photo sharing sites – Instagram and Flickr – are also the two best suited to business use, and the ones we shall focus on in this chapter.

Are these sites repositories for our images (content tools); or social networks in their own right (outreach tools)? Images are a form of content that can be shared with social networks. While Flickr and Instagram may be thought of as social networks, since people can 'like' or 'favourite' images and comment on them, and even join groups and discussions on Flickr, this is really an added bonus to your core networks. The important thing is to have some interesting content to engage your audience with, and reach them in the greatest numbers on the networks they use. By using Instagram and Flickr you are already reaching the people who use those sites. By sharing those images on more generic social networks such as Facebook and Twitter you can also engage your fans and followers with content.

You can, of course, also post images directly on many social networks, including Facebook, Twitter and Google+. But it makes sense to use a photo sharing site and repost your images to social networks from there. You are then reaching the widest possible audience across your networks, and it will save you time, since you can post the same image to multiple networks – often automatically, as you upload it.

Why does photo sharing work for business?

Businesses are embracing photo sharing. According to research by social analytics firm Simply Measured, more than half of top brands were on Instagram by the end of 2012 – within two years of its launch. Photo sharing as a business tool harnesses the power of images, the influence and reach of social media – and the increasing ubiquity of camera phones.

Businesses are embracing photo sharing.

The web is a more visual place than ever, and images are essential if you want to compete in today's attention economy. Images are one of the most viral forms of content. If you want your message to be passed on, illustrating it with an attractive image is a good way to increase your chances. Images are powerful because they:

→ get your message across quickly;
→ provoke intuitive, emotional reactions;
→ allow your business to present a human face;
→ encourage more click-throughs than text.

Photo sharing works best if you have a visual element to your business that people are likely to search for on the photo sharing sites they use. It is probably less useful for a service industry, such as accountancy. For example, if you run a hotel in a scenic part of the country, uploading local images will make you findable by people searching for that location. If you run a pet store, there are currently 16,000 Flickr groups dedicated to pets!

Like other forms of social media, photo sharing works best if you get involved in the community. Just as you can increase your visibility in the blogosphere by commenting on other people's posts, you will be more visible if you comment on other people's photos, 'like' or 'favourite' them, take part in discussions within Flickr groups or use hashtags on Instagram. Together with uploading some great photos of your own, this social activity will lead people on to your profile page – which is the one place you really can sell yourself. Use this to write about your business and link to your website – but keep other commercial activity to a minimum. The focus should be on meaningful interactions based on the photographs. Think of Flickr and Instagram as a community-building platform – a way to engage and involve your customers through sharing and commenting on photos.

Photo sharing in action

How a fashion brand engages with Instagram in Brazil

Levi's Brazil (**www.levi.com.br**) was an early adopter of Instagram marketing, in a country that is one of the fastest-growing social media markets in the world. According to a 2012 comScore report, more than 46 million Brazilians are online and 97 per cent of those use social media.

Photo sharing sites are great for promoting your brand visually to engage fans without being as obvious as selling directly – and the 'cool' of Instagram is a great fit with fashion brands, many of whom are now using it. With over 10,000 followers and 900 images at **instagram.com/levisbrasil**, Levi's Brazil use it to post not only styled photos of models but also images of people wearing Levi's clothing. By including hashtags such as #streetstyle, #instafashion and #denim they make these findable by a wider audience, and collate them by theme. They also show new clothing that will be included in upcoming collections, tagging images with, for example, #newcollection or #fallwinter2013, to give followers previews of yet-to-be-released products. But it's not all clothing: they also post images that reflect the brand's personality. All their posts make full use of Instagram's retro filters which are a perfect match with the Levi's look.

Get the idea: You don't need to be a big fashion brand to benefit from Instagram marketing. Anything visual, from food to events to travel can work well. Bear in mind the style of various imaged-based platforms: Instagram has a certain urban, funky, retro vibe, whereas Pinterest images tend to look like they're clipped from glossy lifestyle magazines. Communicate your style and brand personality with images, and tag them to make them more findable. Give users a reason to follow you – in this case exclusive previews of forthcoming collections. What information can your followers gain access to only by following you?

Get up to speed with photo sharing

We will look in more detail at how you might use Instagram and Flickr for the rest of this chapter. The steps to follow are as follows:

→ Sign up to Instagram and/or Flickr.

→ Upload some photos.

→ Start a Flickr group.

→ Link to other social media.

Instagram or Flickr?

Which photo sharing site is right for you? Or should you use both? In terms of sheer numbers, both sites have broadly similar web traffic, according to 2013 Alexa rankings. They also have a similar age demographic. But Instagram has twice the users of Flickr.

→ **Instagram** – 130 million registered users, 4 billion images uploaded (2013); largest demographic: 25–34-year-olds.

→ **Flickr** – 90 million registered users (2013), 6 billion images uploaded, 80 milion unique visitors pcm (2011); largest demographic: 'Millennials, men 18–34 and affluents' according to Yahoo (**http://advertising.yahoo.com/article/flickr.html**).

Since Flickr updated its website and app in 2013, both services look remarkably similar, and both have a homepage 'news feed' that displays the latest photos from people you follow. Both sites also allow you to tag people who appear in your photos, and to upload video clips as well as images.

Which site seems to have the most interest in your niche?

A useful starting point is to search both for keywords in your topic area. Which site seems to have the most interest in your niche? You can also experiment with both and see which works best, or which you prefer to use; and you can also have the best of both worlds by linking your Instagram account to Flickr, so that those Instagram images you want to share on Flickr too are shared there automatically.

Instagram

Instagram is a smartphone app available for iPhone and Android. It allows users to take photos, apply a digital filter to them, upload them to their account and share them on various social networks including Twitter and Facebook. Users can 'follow' each other's photostreams, and like and comment on other photos. As of June 2013, users can also upload up to 15 seconds of video. Comments and descriptions can include @usernames and hashtags that become clickable links – rather like Twitter.

Why use Instagram?

→ It has become the app of choice for sharing smartphone photos via social networks.

→ It is backed by the world's largest social network: Facebook.

On Instagram users tend to browse the feed of photos from people they follow. Whenever an Instagram user browses their feed, so long as they are following you, this is a marketing opportunity for you – *if* your images are relevant and interesting enough.

Instagram also has a number of third-party apps that allow you to do more with the service and measure your results. One of the most useful is Statigram (**http://statigr.am**), which includes plenty of metrics on your Instagram account, and some ways to promote it, including by generating a feed of images for your Facebook page or blog.

To join Instagram: simply download the app, create an account and start following some people.

Flickr

Flickr also allows video sharing (up to 90 seconds and 500MB per file) as well as photo sharing. Images can be organised into sets and collections, tagged with keywords, geotagged, and shared on other networks. Although overt commercial use of Flickr is against their terms of service, you can still use it to engage your community online and lead them back to your website.

Instagram may have twice the users, but Flickr is fighting back, partly thanks to an own goal by Instagram. At the end of 2012, Instagram updated its terms of use to allow it the right to sell users' photos to third parties without notification or compensation. This controversial policy was quickly dropped – but not before damage had been done to the brand. The rise and rise of Instagram abruptly halted as outraged users switched to other services, notably Flickr, which released a new iPhone app with built-in vintage filters to rival Instagram. This may be a short-term blip – but the new app will have long-term benefit for Flickr because, partly thanks to Instagram, we like to upload photos from our phones now.

The new Flickr app and its redesigned website also make browsing the feed of your contacts – and groups – much more intuitive and easy than it previously was, giving it more of an Instagram-style community feel.

To join Flickr: Flickr was acquired by Yahoo! in 2005, and you will need a Yahoo! login to get started – but this can be set up easily within minutes. The service is free to use, or $24.95 (about £16) for a 'Pro' account with unlimited storage. When setting up your account, include a description of yourself and your business on your profile – and make sure you include a profile photo, or 'buddy icon' – it's a real turn-off on Flickr if you don't. This could be your company logo.

Upload some photos

Now that you've joined Instagram and/or Flickr, the next step is to upload some images.

One reason why photo sharing has taken off in recent years is the development of smartphone technology. I have used Flickr pretty much since it launched, but I have always used a digital SLR camera to take pictures, save them to my desktop computer and upload them to the site from there. Until recently it wouldn't have occurred to me to take pictures with my phone. But smartphone cameras have improved in quality to the extent that more and more people are happy to use them to take and upload photos. High-speed networks mean it is now easy for many of us to upload images directly from our phones on the move. And the range of filters and effects such as spot-focus on Instagram – and now on the Flickr app – means it is almost impossible to take a bad photo.

You can share photos easily in a few clicks from your phone wherever you are.

So you can share photos easily in a few clicks from your phone wherever you are. But *what* should you share? Whether you use Instagram and/or Flickr, the same principles apply: engage your community with images that tell your business story and communicate your brand, rather than simply cataloguing your products. Think about images that would provoke positive feelings about your brand. 'Relatability' is important – think of images you can share that people can relate to on a human level. Examples include:

→ Photos of you or your staff in action – giving a seminar, arranging flowers, rewiring a house, catering events, making a cappuccino, selling sweets, restoring furniture – whatever it is that you do.

→ Images of your products – although you should avoid using photo sharing sites purely as product catalogues, there's no reason not to include image of your cakes, wine, jewellery, etc. It is likely you will find Flickr groups relating to your specific product and you should add these images where the group rules allow you to.

→ Products being used by your customers. This can be a fun way to engage your community and can be combined with hashtags and contests on Instagram.

→ Sneak previews of products that are about to launch. As I write this, a publisher friend has just posted an image of a couple of book jackets on Instagram with the description: 'Beautiful new books, hot off the press. Out in May.'

→ Images of events, workshops or seminars you run, or any other community activities, from industry conferences to tweetups. Always make sure if you are photographing people that they are happy for their picture to be used.

→ Photos that share company news, such as new employees or new products.

→ Photos that show us your business 'behind the scenes', such as the people behind your company, how your products are made, or simply what your office/shop/boat building yard looks like.

Essential things to do when adding photos include:

→ **Describe it** – add a short description, as much as you need to tell us what is going on, but avoid a sales pitch. You can include weblinks on Flickr – but overly commercial use is discouraged. You can include them on Instagram too, but they won't be clickable, so this is slightly pointless (although when a description containing a link is pushed through to Twitter or Facebook, it will become clickable there). Descriptions and comments on Instagram can also include @usernames, rather like Twitter, for example to mention other Instagram users who are in a photo or to address people directly in comments.

→ **Title it** – on Flickr you will also need to add a title. The default title will be whatever the filename of your image is – which might be as meaningless as 'IMG0001254.jpg' if you're uploading direct from your camera.

→ **Tag it** – give your photo some descriptive tags on Flickr, one of which should be your business name where relevant. On both Flickr and Instagram you can tag people who appear in your photos. On Instagram, hashtags are a popular way to tag images with keywords – such as #streetphotography, #travel, #cupcakes or #books. These become clickable links that display other images using the same hashtags – very similar to the way they are used on Twitter. Think of inventive ways you can use hashtags, not only to tag the content of your images but to build community, for example with hashtag contests (see FAQ) or by starting your own unique hashtag in the way that NH Hoteles created #wakeuppics.

→ **Geotag it** – this is essential for any business where location is important, such as tourism, travel or real estate. But it is also useful for any business with a physical location. This is a subtle way to help people find you without being overtly promotional: upload some pictures of your restaurant, geotag them, and then people can click on the location link that appears next to your photo to find you! On Flickr a link will appear under your image on its single photo page inviting you to 'Add this photo to your map!' or listing its location. Clicking on this will show your photo on a map, and people can click a link to **See nearby photos and videos** if they want to see other images taken at that location. Be sure to include the name of the location in your tags too, as this will help people who search for a location to find your image. On Instagram, the location function is integrated with foursquare, and the location can only be clicked on in the phone app (rather than the website). This again displays a map of where your image was taken, followed by more images taken at that location by others.

All these things will help your photos to be found on photo sharing sites and in search engines.

The way in which you upload images is a little different on Instagram and Flickr. On Flickr you can upload via the website or your phone. With Instagram, although you can use the website, it has less functionality than the smartphone app, and you can only upload images from your phone.

Uploading to Instagram

Images are uploaded to Instagram via the smartphone app (available for iPhone or Android). Once you have downloaded it, it's a simple matter of tapping the camera icon at the bottom and taking a photo.

You can then edit it. This the stage where you can use what Instagram is best known for – its vintage filters. You don't have to add a filter effect, but around 60 per cent of users do. There are other editing options too, such as adding a spot focus.

The final upload stage includes options to share your image on various social networks – which is where Instagram becomes a more powerful outreach tool. Your photo then appears on your profile page and in your photostream – and in the feeds of people who follow you.

You can also upload images from your phone's camera roll instead of a photo you have just taken. Tap the camera icon, but instead of the shutter button press the small image from your photo library that appears next to it. Scroll through your images, choose one, scale and crop if you wish – or just leave it as it is (but press the crop button regardless). Then you can edit, upload and share your image as if you had just taken it.

Uploading to Flickr

For a while Flickr has enabled users to upload images from their phones via email. But the Flickr app is the best way to do this now. The latest Flickr app works in pretty much the same way as Instagram, including a range of filters.

With Flickr, you also have another option – to upload via the website. If you have a lot of images, this can save you time by batch-processing your uploads. The built-in upload function (**www.flickr.com/upload**) allows you to drag and drop images, or select them from your hard drive. You can then add titles, descriptions and tags as a batch or individually. You can also organise your photos into 'sets' which can in turn be combined into 'collections'.

The final thing you need to decide on when uploading images to Flickr is the level of visibility for your images, and how they can be used. You can set account defaults for these, but also amend them for any individual image any time.

→ **Public or private?** You can make photos visible to everyone, just to you, or just to friends and/or family. This can be useful if you use the same account for personal as well as business photos, and just want the business ones to be public.

→ **Copyright or Creative Commons?** The default on Flickr is that you own the copyright to all your images, and '© All Rights Reserved' is displayed next to them. You can, however, change this, and opt for Creative Commons. This is an alternative to copyright, and means you can allow others to use your images so long as they use them in the way you want – such as for non-commercial use, unmodified, and with a credit.

Start a Flickr group

A great way to engage other people on Flickr is with groups. There are plenty of groups for anything you can imagine – search for some to join in your topic area. Do you sell cakes? There are about 8,000 groups for that! If you are a local business, there is probably a group for your town or city too, which will help you reach a local audience.

There are plenty of groups for anything you can imagine.

Observe the group posting rules, which vary from group to group and are set by the group administrator. But then get uploading. Joining groups is the main way to raise awareness of your images. Be sure to take part in any forum discussions in your chosen groups, and comment on other members' photos – particularly those that get a lot of views.

The other option is to create your own group. You might create a group for your business that only you post to; or you could create an open group that others can post to. This is a more engaging way to build connections, and encourages user-generated content – and therefore cuts down on your workload. This approach would be suitable for any events or seminars that you organise. You can also include discussion forums in your group, an additional way of communicating with and engaging your members.

Once you have set up a Flickr group pool you can then also pull images contributed to it back into your blog or website using a widget.

Frequently asked questions

What are hashtag contests?

Hashtag contests have become a popular way to engage people on Instagram. These work by asking people to upload images on a specific theme and tag them with a hashtag – and possibly with your @username as well. You then judge the winner(s) from those that get the most likes and/or that you judge to be the best – and award a prize. To get a sense of what hashtag contests look like, visit **http://statigr.am/contest-ongoing.php** to see some current ones. You can use Statigram to manage and run contests (see **http://statigr.am/contest-discover.php**), or simply do it yourself, monitor entries manually, and get the word out via your Instagram profile and other social media channels. You don't have to offer an expensive prize either – you could simply repost the winning entries on your account as a way of rewarding the winners with a bit of extra exposure, especially if you have a large following. This is not a feature built in to Instagram, but can be done with an app called 'Repost for Instagram'. By using hashtags relevant to your brand to run photo contests you can engage and reward your customers.

Link to other social media

Instagram

One of the great advantages of Instagram is that it is built to enable sharing to other social networks. The options are Facebook, Twitter, email, Tumblr, Flickr and foursquare. Connect to the sites and services you want by tapping the cog icon in the top right of your profile screen, and then choosing **Share Settings**. Posting is not automatic to the networks you choose: you can choose which network(s) you want to post an image to each time you upload one – so you can keep your content relevant to your communities. You can also share images later that you have previously uploaded – apart from on Flickr and foursquare, where you can only share when you first upload an image.

Linking Instagram to Facebook is a good idea, since you can choose to post to your profile or to your business page. Both now have 'timeline' layouts, which give greater weight to images, and the square images generated by Instagram look good on Facebook.

Flickr

The Flickr app works in a similar way to Instagram, except that the sharing options are Facebook, Twitter, Tumblr or email. Choose which network you want to post to when you upload from mobile.

The other way of linking to social networks from Flickr is via your profile settings on the website:

→ Hover over your buddy icon and choose **Settings**.

→ Click the **Sharing & Extending** tab.

→ Choose which sites you want to connect to, from Facebook, Twitter, Tumblr, Blogger, LiveJournal and WordPress.

Quick win

Pull images onto your Facebook page or blog with a widget

With either Instagram or Flickr you can pull your photos into your Facebook page, blog, website. As well as adding some content, this gives people who are already on Instagram or Flickr the opportunity to click through and add you as a contact, or see the rest of your images. It is another way to build a community around your business by going where your customers are.

→ **Facebook pages**: Use Flickr Tab (**www.facebook.com/flickrtabapp**) to pull Flickr images into your Facebook page, and use Statigram to create an Instagram feed tab for your Facebook page (**http://statigr.am/promote.php**).

→ **Blogs/Websites**: Use Statigram to create an Instagram widget to pull images into your blog or website – or try a WordPress plugin such as Instagram for WordPress (**http://wordpress.org/extend/plugins/instagram-for-wordpress**) or Simply Instagram (**http://wordpress.org/extend/plugins/simply-instagram**). There are also several Flickr WordPress plugins. Try Awesome Flickr Gallery (**http://wordpress.org/extend/plugins/awesome-flickr-gallery-plugin**).

Manage the workload

Instagram

→ **Use third-party tools**. It's not always very easy to manage your account via the Instagram website. Save yourself time by using a service that enables you to see and search for photos and followers easily, such as Statigram or Nitrogram.

→ **Share to Flickr**. Connect to your Flickr account in your share settings. This saves you posting to both, and gives you the best of both worlds by posting selected Instagram images direct to your Flickr photostream.

Flickr

→ **Upload in bulk**. Use the Flickr Desktop Uploadr (download from **www.flickr.com/tools**) – a piece of software for Mac or PC that sits on your desktop and is useful for managing larger volumes of uploads – even whole folders of images.

→ **Encourage user-generated content**. Use a public Flickr Group and encourage people to post to it according to moderation rules you specify. Suitable uses for this might include coverage of events – something media140 do to cover their worldwide social media conferences, for example (**www.flickr.com/groups/media140**), resulting in around 1,600 photos from 90 members. This approach also creates content that you can pull back onto your blog automatically with a widget that displays the latest uploads in your sidebar.

Measure your results

Instagram

Instagram has a lot of third-party apps to help you with analytics. These are useful because, since Instagram is more of a social network, you want stats not just on your images but on your followers. With all of these services, just visit the websites and sign in with your Instagram account.

- → Statigram – **http://statigr.am**
- → Extragram – **http://extragr.am**
- → Nitrogram – **http://nitrogr.am**
- → Gramfeed – **www.gramfeed.com**

Try them out, and see which works for you. They are all useful for viewing your feed, finding people to follow and – importantly – tracking your results. These tools can offer valuable insights into the best times to post photos based on user engagement and help you identify your most active followers. These tend to be the ones who help you spread the word, so make sure you keep them engaged.

Flickr

If you have a Flickr Pro account, you get access to loads of statistics on your account. Just go to 'Stats' under the 'You' menu to see a graph of views of your account over time and find your most viewed photos. You can also see where your traffic is coming from in the Referrers list, and a handy breakdown of details of all your photos and videos on Flickr, such as what proportion are tagged, geotagged or have comments. Finally, if you want to measure click-throughs to your website as a result of your activity on Flickr, make your weblink from your profile page a unique URL that refers on to your site.

Photosharing best practice

1 **Post images regularly**. On Flickr, you can afford to be a bit more ad hoc about posting images. On Instagram, however, it is good practice to post regularly to keep your followers engaged. Don't bunch a load of images together, though, as this can be annoying to followers. Spreading your images out also means they are more likely to be seen by more followers, who will typically dip in and out of their photostream.

2 **Post interesting images**. Focus less on images of your products and more on lifestyle photos that are visually appealing and that people will want to engage with.

3 **Tag your images** – add Flickr tags to anything that a Flickr visitor might search on that would lead them to your photo; use hashtags in Instagram image descriptions.

4 **Be sociable**. Participate in the photo sharing culture and community rather than focusing too much on marketing. Engage in brief exchanges through comments on both Instagram and Flickr. On Instagram you can also use hashtags and @usernames, just like you can on Twitter.

5 **Create your own hashtag** – and engage people that use it. On Instagram you can search for and collate images using hashtags. Start a hashtag that is unique to you and invite people to join in. The consistent use by NH Hoteles (**instagram.com/nh_hoteles**) of #wakeuppics to post sunrises – and inviting others to do the same – is a great example of this. What started as a photo contest became a theme that continues to engage followers. It even has its own microsite at **www.wakeuppics.com**.

6 **Run photo contests**. These are popular on Instagram and a great way of involving your community. Have followers submit photos to a themed hashtag, judge them, and repost to celebrate the winners using the 'Repost for Instagram' app.

7 **Use your images on your blog**. Use your Flickr or Instagram accounts as a source of images for your blog – and link back to them. Use an image on every blog post so that it is 'pinnable' by others on Pinterest.

8 **Pull in Flickr group photos** onto your blog using a widget. This showcases your Flickr account and encourages people to submit their images to your group pool.

9 **Upload video too** – although we've focused on images in this chapter, don't forget that you can also upload short video clips to Flickr and Instagram.

10 **Use your smartphone** – upload on the move to keep your feed fresh and your content relevant and immediate.

Take action

→ **Join** Flickr and/or Instagram.

→ **Upload** some interesting, relevant images.

→ **Join** Flickr groups relevant to your topic – then start your own.

→ **Run** a hashtag contest on Instagram to boost engagement.

→ **Link** your Flickr and Instagram accounts to Facebook, Twitter and other social networks.

→ **Embed** your Instagram or Flickr photos back on your Facebook page, blog or website to engage people there too.

Get out there

Part Four

Build an online community

How to choose and use social networks

Chapter Ten

If blogging has made everyone a publisher, social networking has made everyone a celebrity. Social networking sites have revolutionised the way we use the web. On today's internet, if you don't have what William Gibson has called a 'home-built media persona', you don't exist. This applies to businesses as well as individuals. Like it or not, in the social media age you are a public figure with a reputation to protect and a brand to communicate. Do it with authenticity and personality, and you can build an army of loyal fans.

Social networking has made everyone a celebrity.

Three things you need as a business are influence, profile and reach. The social media revolution has made it possible for anyone to achieve this through the ability to publish content online. Content is the starting point – but social networks are how you promote that content and get the word out.

In this chapter, we shall look at the case for social networking, and some principles that apply whichever one you choose. The social networks that are likely to be of most benefit to your business are Facebook, LinkedIn, Twitter, Google+ and Pinterest, and we shall look at these in more depth in the following chapters.

What is social networking?

Although there is a wide variety of social networking sites, and new ones continue to spring up and catch on, many share some common features, including the ability to:

→ Create a personal profile with some information about yourself, usually including a website and a profile image or 'avatar'.

→ Update your 'status' – a short description of what you're doing.

→ Tag your status or content with your location.

→ Add friends to your list of contacts or follow other accounts.

→ Set up a group, page, circle or list of people who share your area of interest.

- → Create and manage events.
- → Add and share photos and video.
- → Access extra functions such as metrics through third-party applications.
- → Promote your product or service with advertising.

Social networks may have started as places for individuals to connect with each other, but it has become obvious that businesses want to use social media for marketing. And the major social networks have responded with new business features, including:

- → **Facebook pages** are now the default way in which businesses and brands engage people on Facebook – now not only via pages, but with customised pages.
- → **LinkedIn company pages** are a newer addition to what was always a business-orientated network, and rolled out with a new look at the end of 2012.
- → **Twitter** has always had a mix of personal and business accounts, but new services targeting businesses advertising have been introduced, including 'promoted tweets'.
- → **Google+ business pages** launched in 2011, with a similar look and many of the same functions as personal profiles.
- → **Pinterest business accounts** launched at the end of 2012.

Why social networking works for business

Social networks are the entry point of your sales funnel. They are the medium through which potential customers first become aware of you. If you can engage them with the useful, valuable, pass-on-able content you created in Part 3, you can convert them to fans, friends and followers – and a proportion of them to email subscribers too. It's all about encouraging people to pass through your sales funnel. Reach people with social networks, engage them with social media content, and use calls to action to encourage them onto your website – where you can sell them stuff.

Social networks are a good starting point because so many people use them, and spend so much of their time there. About a fifth of our online time is spent on a social network, and it continues to rise – up 38 per cent between 2011 and 2012 according to Nielsen Media, more than any other online activity. Part of the reason for this continued growth is the widespread take-up of smartphones, and the proliferation of social networking apps on them. If your business doesn't have a presence on social networks, you're missing a massive opportunity to reach people where they are – whether online or on their phones.

Social networking works for business because you can build connections, build your reputation, build a list, build word of mouth and build trust. All are key ingredients for online marketing success, and nothing beats social networks for making it happen.

→ **Build connections**. Like real-life face-to-face networking, you can meet people and start conversations online. Unlike real-life networking, you don't have to do this one-to-one, but one-to-many. Very many. You can reach more people, all over the world, 24 hours a day, articulate your offering to them and collect their contact details without ever leaving your office.

→ **Build your reputation**. You can become well known in your niche community, and the obvious 'go to' person on your area of expertise for the people you want to reach.

→ **Build a list**. Your networks act as opted-in mailing lists you can use to reach highly targeted people who are likely to be interested in your product or service. They've sought you out and chosen to be on your list, after all.

→ **Build word of mouth**. Word of mouth marketing becomes much easier to achieve with the power of social networking. If you create content worth passing on, your fans will help market your business for you.

→ **Build trust**. As well as getting your message passed on to new people by people they trust, social networks help build trust in you too. People like to do business with people they know; and mediating yourself via a social network is a great way for people to get to know you.

Get Up to Speed with Online Marketing

Creating community

Another important reason why social networks work for business is that they enable you to build a community around your products and services. Building an online community is the single most important thing you can do to grow your business. Members of your community are not simply customers or your 'market niche': they are your fans, your brand ambassadors, your focus group. They are loyal customers who will stay tuned for your latest product, but they will also refer business to their friends, and tell you what they want next. How can you cultivate your own?

Building an online community is the single most important thing you can do to grow your business.

It starts with shifting your focus from your business to your community. Think of your social networking activities not so much as marketing as community-building. Craig Newmark, founder of CraigsList, once said: 'The more you think about business as being a community service, the more successful you become.' What community does your business serve? Spend a bit of time thinking about who, exactly, your community is – and what value you can offer them.

Successful brands and businesses are the ones who find a way into the daily lives of their customers. Social networking is a place where many people spend at least some of their day. They are an excellent way to find – and build – your community.

Building communities around your products is the new way to market your business. But you can turn this on its head and do it the other way around: create products around your community. Start a community in a niche topic area first, build a following, then create the products they want, and sell them back to your (now sizable) group of followers. This is the approach I have taken with Publishing Talk – starting with a niche, topic-based blog, promoting the content with social networks to build a following, then creating products (in my case ebooks, magazines and other learning resources) based on the needs of the community. Starting with communities rather than products is a long-term strategy, though, and means you will need to wait a while before the cash comes in. If you have an existing catalogue of products or range of services, think about pre-existing online communities you can reach as well, while you build up your own.

Social networking in action

How a wedding stationery company grew to a six-figure turnover with social networking

Ivy Ellen Wedding Stationery (**www.ivyellen.co.uk**) is a wedding stationery business based in Brighton, UK. Using a range of social networks, particularly Facebook, Twitter and LinkedIn, it has built up a wealth of useful leads, contacts – and business. Each network is used differently: LinkedIn for professional contact with wedding suppliers such as venues, photographers, dressmakers and wedding planners; Facebook for more customer-focused special offers, wedding freebies and funny wedding stuff; and Twitter for more frequent updates – fun, friendly wedding tips, facts and news. At present Twitter is its most successful social media tool for driving traffic and growing brand awareness.

Ivy Ellen's use of social networking has led to both sales and exposure. The company has won two awards, had several blog posts and articles written about them, won sales leads, had brand champions referring them to others, and is building incoming weblinks, industry knowledge, sales orders and substantial brand awareness – all in a short space of time. Since its launch in 2009 the company has grown to a six-figure turnover, been featured in a British movie, worked on celebrity weddings, won Best Wedding Stationery at the 2013 Wedding Ideas Awards and is now widely recognised in the wedding industry. Social media has been central to its success.

The key is being organised, and setting aside time for marketing. Owner Jeremy Corner says: 'You should focus on spending at least a third of your time marketing – more for a new business in my view.' The company uses a number of third-party tools to help manage the time spent on Twitter, including filtering and scheduling tweets with HootSuite. 'Being connected to your customers and industry peers in a personal way has a fantastic effect on our businesses,' he continues, 'so I consider it time well spent. I would not be growing the Ivy Ellen brand as fast without these tools. If you are consumer facing, social media is a must-have in your toolbox. Just as you should think about what value your business offers your customers, think about what value you can offer your followers. Be helpful, be funny or be informative. Most people will enjoy following and interacting with you if you do these things.'

Get the idea: Use several social networks, but use each in a way appropriate to the platform and its audience. Set aside time for social networking, and use a social media dashboard such as HootSuite to help manage it. Focus on the value you can offer, and your follower numbers will increase.

Top 10 social networking sites

Some of the most significant social networks with potential to use for marketing, in order of registered users as of 2013, are as follows. Some are only relevant to specific geographic markets or age demographics, while others are more widespread and general.

Social network URL	Description	Registered users
Facebook **www.facebook.com**	**Facebook** is the largest and most geographically spread general social network. Pages are now the default way for businesses to engage people on Facebook, ideally with customised 'tabs'.	1 billion+
Twitter **http://twitter.com**	**Twitter** continues to enjoy huge growth. Its size, combined with its user base and real-time nature, make it an important and influential social network.	600 million
Google+ **http://plus.google.com**	**Google+** launched in 2011 and integrates its previous social services with new services such as circles, hangouts and communities.	500 million

▶

Social network URL	Description	Registered users
Habbo **www.habbo.com**	**Habbo** is a general social networking site for teenagers. Has over 31 communities worldwide, and includes chat rooms and user profiles.	268 million
LinkedIn **www.linkedin.com**	**LinkedIn** is a business-orientated social network – a combination of an online CV/résumé and business contact list. You can also join and create groups and set up company pages.	225 million
Instagram **http://instagram.com**	Is **Instagram** a photo sharing site, a smartphone app or a social network? It can usefully be thought of as a place to engage people directly with image-based content. See also Flickr (90 million users).	130 million
Bebo **www.bebo.com**	**Bebo** is a general social network with a younger demographic.	117 million
Tagged **www.tagged.com**	**Tagged** is a California-based social network initially aimed at teens, but now with a more adult demographic.	100 million
Pinterest **http://pinterest.com**	**Pinterest** is a pinboard-style social bookmarking site based on images that are pinned from websites onto themed boards. Launched in 2010, it is growing fast: user numbers increased from 9 million to 40 million in 2012.	70 million+

Get Up to Speed with Online Marketing

MySpace www.myspace.com	Remember **MySpace**? Once the largest social network (2005–2008), its influence diminished as Facebook soared. But it may be set for a comeback – partly thanks to some new backers, notably Justin Timberlake, and a major site re-launch. Tends to have a younger demographic, and found its niche in the promotion of music and other creative work.	50 million

Which social network?

There are lots of social networking sites out there. Which do you choose? Do you just sign up to as many as possible and hope for the best? Do you pick the largest?

The important thing is to go where your market is, as with any social media tool. Do some keyword searches on various social networks. Which ones look likely places to find and engage people who will be interested in your topic?

Go where your market is.

Another factor is geography. While the well-known, generic networks that are used widely across the world are a good starting point, what if you do business in China or Russia? There are a number of networks specific to or popular in geographic markets that you also need to be aware of:

→ **Qzone** (http://qzone.qq.com – 480 million users) is a general social network for users in mainland China. Also available for this market are microblogging site Sina Weibo (300 million users) and Renren (160 million users).

→ **Vkontakte** (http://vk.com – 124 million users), billed as 'the largest European social network', is popular in Russia and former Soviet republics.

→ **Orkut** (**www.orkut.com** – 100 million users) is owned by Google and popular in India and Brazil.

→ **Netlog** (**http://netlog.com** – 98 million users) is popular in Europe, Turkey, the Arab world and Canada's Québec province. Formerly known as Facebox and Redbox.

→ **Friendster** (**www.friendster.com** – 90 million users) is popular in Southeast Asia, but no longer popular in the Western world.

→ **Hi5** (**http://hi5.com** – 80 million users) is popular in Nepal, Mongolia, Romania, Jamaica, Central Africa, Portugal and Latin America – but not very popular in the USA.

A good guiding principle is to focus on the largest networks worldwide, those that are best suited to promoting your business. If you are new to networking, I would start with Facebook and/or Twitter – with a few caveats:

→ Set up a **Facebook** page and a **Twitter** account. In terms of sheer size, it makes sense to be findable here. With such vast user numbers on these sites, there is bound to be a sizeable proportion of users who will be interested in what you have to offer – and there will be a way for you to use these sites effectively. What's more, you can automatically link many other services to Facebook and Twitter, such as your blog and Instagram images.

→ Create a profile on **LinkedIn** – whether or not you use it for networking. It's a way to create an online résumé that you can link to from your website, and you can use LinkedIn to solicit client testimonials. Use LinkedIn more actively if you are a business-to-business (B2B) company.

→ Sign up to **Google+** if only to benefit from better search results when people search for you or your business on Google. Invest more time here if you have multiple market segments you want to reach, since Google+ has a real advantage here.

→ Use **Pinterest** if you have a strong visual element to your business and can post attractive 'lifestyle' images. Pinterest is becoming one of the biggest sources of referral traffic.

Get Up to Speed with Online Marketing

→ If you do business in a territory that has its own local language social network, or where other networks are popular, establish a presence on the largest social network in the region(s) in which you do business.

→ If you work in the creative industries – such as music or film – set up a profile on **MySpace**, which has found its niche in this area.

→ If you want to target a younger demographic, **Habbo** is specifically for teens and **Bebo** attracts a younger audience.

Choose one or two large generic networks as your primary network. You can set up a profile on all of them of course, even if it is just a 'holding' page that directs people to your main social networking profile. This in itself is useful, since findability is key in online marketing. People may search for you on the networks they use; but Google searches will also show results from social networking sites high up the results page, since these sites are so highly ranked themselves.

The other reason for setting up accounts, even if you're not ready to use them yet, is to secure your name. Registering usernames on social networking sites is a bit like registering domain names. If your business, brand or personal name is available as a username, register it quickly before someone else does.

It also pays to think carefully about what you call your Twitter account, Facebook page, Pinterest account and so on. Depending on how you are best known, this might be your business name, personal name or a topic-based name. Think about not just which search terms people will use to find you: think about what topics people in your community of interest might search for. This could even influence your choice of business name or strapline, if you are just setting up. For example, one of the reasons my @publishingtalk Twitter account has taken off in the way it has is because whenever someone searches Twitter for the word 'publishing' it is one of the first accounts that comes up.

Location-based networking

What if you are a local business? You can benefit from using these networks to engage your local client base too – and take advantage of location tagging that is available on many networks, including

Facebook, Twitter, Google+ and Instagram. But you may also want to use a specific location-based network. The most popular of these is foursquare (**http://foursquare.com**), with over 30 million users worldwide.

" You may also want to use a specific location-based network.

Launched in 2009, foursquare adds a real-world dimension to social networking that can help bricks-and-mortar businesses reach out to new customers. It allows users to connect with friends, update their location and 'check in' at venues using the smartphone app. They are awarded points, earn badges and are crowned the 'Mayor' of venues they visit more than other users. Notifications can be pushed through to Facebook and Twitter.

Foursquare provides services for businesses through its Merchant Platform (**http://foursquare.com/business**), which is used by over a million businesses. Business tools include 'local updates' and 'specials', used to tell customers about special promotions, rewards, upcoming events or new offerings.

Frequently asked questions

I'm uncomfortable about opening my personal life to the world. Do I really need a personal profile?
Business pages and accounts are a way around having personal profiles. But don't underestimate the power of personality and your personal brand. Human beings are more trusted than faceless businesses, and your social networking presence should be more than a sanitised corporate version of yourself. When people decide whether to connect on social networks, knowing who the person is in real life is a big deciding factor for many people – 63 per cent, according to research by Nielsen Media. So don't hide yourself away. If you have business accounts, consider including links to personal accounts too where you have them – for example in your Twitter biographies.

Manage the workload

We will look at managing the workload for individual networks in the following chapters. But one important way to manage the workload across all your social networks is to use a social media dashboard. Two of the best known are TweetDeck (**www.tweetdeck.com**) and HootSuite (**http://hootsuite.com**).

TweetDeck is a web-based service, desktop app or smartphone app that allows you to manage multiple Twitter accounts plus Facebook updates from the same dashboard. It can also be used to set up keyword searches and schedule tweets in advance. It was acquired by Twitter in 2011, controversially dropping its support for other social networks such as LinkedIn, foursquare and MySpace in the process.

HootSuite is a web-based dashboard and social media management system. Also available as a smartphone app, it supports multiple Twitter accounts, plus Facebook, LinkedIn, Google+, foursquare and more. It allows pre-scheduling of updates, and even 'AutoScheduling' at a time for maximum impact. If you have a Pro account, you can also 'bulk schedule' updates by uploading a CSV file. HootSuite also enables teams to manage multiple accounts, collaborate and communicate. Together with powerful analytics available to Pro users, these functions make it popular with organisations – but it is also a brilliant tool for small businesses and entrepreneurs. You can 'create an organisation' and invite people to collaborate with you on updates and more. But you don't have to be a large organisation to benefit from this feature – it might just be you and your virtual assistant or part-time freelancer. Now that TweetDeck has dropped support for most non-Twitter networks, HootSuite should be your first port of call for a tool to manage your social networking.

Measure your results

Your web analytics will give you a good idea of which social networks are driving the most traffic to your site. In addition, there are metrics specific to each social networks, and we shall look at these in the following chapters.

But if you want detailed analytics and reporting on your social networks, upgrade your free HootSuite account to HootSuite Pro ($9.99 per month). These include Google Analytics, Facebook Insights, Influence Scores and Ow.ly Click Summary (ow.ly is HootSuite's URL shortening service). Use HootSuite analytics to track keywords, listen to and engage with your audience; measure your social media return on investment (ROI); and evaluate and measure the influence of social media users. What's more, you can generate detailed reports to share with your team or provide you with the feedback you need to determine if a campaign is working. Once set up, you can schedule these to be automatically emailed to you – and your team, if you wish – at regular intervals.

Influence is a softer measure, but one that can be measured with Klout (**http://klout.com**). Go to the website, connect with the social networks you use, and get a Klout score. This is also useful for spotting and engaging influencers in your niche. Klout for Business (**http://klout. com/s/business**) is now also available, with a dashboard that tells you at a glance whether you are engaging your influencers on the networks where they are most actively exerting their influence, plus which topics your audience influences others on, helping you to focus your efforts.

Social networking best practice

We will look at best practice for individual networks in the following chapters. However, there are a few key principles to bear in mind that apply to all networks:

1 **Post often** – at least once a day on each network you are a member of to maintain interest and reap the marketing benefit.

2 **Post pictures** – social media is highly visual now. Use photos and videos to take advantage of this.

3 **Pass it on** – don't just post your own updates and content – retweet, repin and reshare other people's posts too. They will appreciate it, as will your community if you focus on sharing posts that you think will interest or benefit them. And it will encourage other people to share your posts too.

4 **Be sociable** – this is social media, after all. Reply to people at least some of the time, and comment on other people's posts.

Take action

→ **Register** for accounts with **Facebook** and **Twitter** as a minimum.

→ **Set up** accounts on **LinkedIn**, **Google+** and **Pinterest** – even if you don't intend to use these right away.

→ **Focus** on networks that are a good fit with your business and the community you are trying to reach.

→ **Create** an account on HootSuite to manage your social networking – and consider a Pro account to measure your results.

Find fans on Facebook

How to harness the world's largest network

Chapter Eleven

Facebook is the big success story of the social media revolution. For many people it is part of their daily lives – and a place where they spend at least some of their time every week, either on the website or the smartphone app. And there are a lot of them: over one billion monthly active users. That's not only half the online population – it's a significant chunk of the world population. Your customers are on Facebook – so you need to be. What prospects, leads and opportunities are you missing out on if you're not? But it is not size alone that makes Facebook a good place to do business. Its functions and features lend themselves to finding and engaging your community of interest.

For many people, Facebook *is* social networking.

What is Facebook?

For many people, Facebook *is* social networking. If they are only on one social network, this is likely to be it. The main features of Facebook are as follows. We will look at some of these in more depth, and how you might use them strategically for your business, in this chapter.

→ **Personal profiles**. Unlike Twitter, Google+ and Pinterest, Facebook is a 'closed' network, meaning individual friend requests must be approved before people can interact via personal profiles.

→ **Timelines**. Facebook content is organised into 'timelines' on both profiles and pages, with the most recent posts at the top. Content can include status updates, links, life events and media such as photos and video.

→ **Photos and video**. The timeline layout gives images greater prominence. Captions, locations and dates can be added – and people who appear in photos can be tagged.

→ **Messages**. Facebook messages are organised into 'conversations' and comprise a mix of messages, emails, chats and text messages.

→ **News Feed**. This is a real-time feed of latest 'stories' from a Facebook user's network – including the latest updates and postings from friends, pages, groups and events.

- → **Pages**. Facebook isn't just about profiles. For businesses, it is all about pages, which look remarkably similar to profiles – including the same timeline layout and prominent header image.

- → **Groups**. Facebook encourages the use of groups as private spaces within Facebook for people to discuss common interests.

- → **Events**. Use events to organise your events, manage invitations and send notifications and reminders. Events can be created by people, pages and groups.

- → **Social Ads**. Facebook adverts can be useful for targeting specific demographics on Facebook. They often include additional social information, such as which of your friends have liked a page that is being advertised.

Why Facebook works for business

Over one billion people 'like' and 'comment' an average of 3.2 billion times every day. If your business is not on Facebook, you are excluded from that daily conversation and missing out on the best kind of word-of-mouth marketing: recommendations between friends.

Facebook has become one of the most widely used online marketing tools for business – and that's largely because of the numbers. Because it has such a large user base, you will almost certainly find a community of interest on Facebook, however niche your area. You can reach very specific, targeted users for little cost with 'Social Ads'. You can also pay to promote posts or sponsor stories. But you don't *have* to pay for anything on Facebook: it's completely free to create a page or group specifically for your business or product, and your target market will find it.

When someone 'likes' a page, the updates from that page are included in their news feed – and the fact that they have liked your page may show up in the news feeds of their friends. Facebook users can like individual pieces of content from pages. When someone likes or comments on a page post, that activity may also be shared with their friends, increasing your page's reach. In fact, about 30 per cent of the content of news feeds is from pages rather than profiles. This is how you will use Facebook to promote your business: by creating a page, encouraging people to 'like' it – and then keeping them engaged with content that will appear in their news feeds. Keep them engaged with great content, and your brand will stay in their line of sight on Facebook: as part of their news feed.

Businesses on Facebook have, until now, been very focused on building up the number of 'likes' of their pages. This is understandable, as it's the way to build a list of people you can reach on the social network where they spend so much of their time. But Facebook becomes a more valuable tool when you go beyond building a fan base. Think about engaging and retaining fans – and converting them to members of your email list and paying customers.

Go beyond building a fan base.

Facebook in action

How a cheesecake company converted Facebook fans to paying customers

The English Cheesecake Company (**www.englishcheesecake.com**) wanted to increase sales coming directly from Facebook, build brand awareness, and use Facebook as a platform for developing and launching new products.

Their approach included using Facebook for customer service, engaging fans through polls and feedback, and setting up a Facebook shop. They also used Facebook Ads and Sponsored Stories to grow their fan numbers and connect with new customers, using precise interests such as 'cheesecake' and 'bakery' to reach their target audience, predominantly targeting their core demographic of UK-based females aged 25 to 35.

They set a goal of at least doubling fan growth, yet saw an 11-fold increase in their Facebook fans from 2,000 to 23,000 in one year, with 4,500 likes delivered through Sponsored Stories alone – and 30 per cent of new customers now come through Facebook.

Engaging fans with content is key to their long-term success. Brand and marketing manager Anna Konieczny says: 'For us, creating engaging content that resonate with our fans is a winner. People respond to high quality, delicious-looking images of our products and that encourages sharing between friends. Competitions and various brand partnerships have worked very well for us too: they increase brand awareness and stimulate purchase in the longer term.'

Get the idea: Create engaging content that your target market will want to share. Use niche terms to target ads to keep the cost down. Sell products directly from your Facebook page by installing a shop on one of your tabs (sometimes called 'F-Commerce'). The English Cheesecake Company used Storefront Social for this (**http://storefrontsocial.com**).

Sources: **www.facebook.com/business/theenglishcheesecakecompany** *and The English Cheesecake Company*

Get up to speed with Facebook

The main step you need to take to benefit from Facebook marketing is to create, customise and promote your business page – and that is what we shall focus on in this section. But we will also look at some other strategies worth considering too.

→ Create and customise a page as your main Facebook marketing tool.

→ Engage people with updates.

→ Promote your page.

→ Create a Facebook group.

→ Create a Facebook event to engage your community in real life.

Create a Facebook page

You can start off on Facebook by setting up a page – but only if you don't already have a profile and don't intend to create one. But I would strongly recommend you create a profile first, even if you only use it for creating pages. You can always control who sees your content via the privacy settings – and you may be surprised how much business comes your way via your personal profile.

Be sure to add a brief biography, your business web address under **Contact information** and your current business under **Work and education**. Ideally, this will link to your business Facebook page, as people will then be able to click through to it from the **About** section at the top of your profile.

Then start setting up your page: just go to **www.facebook.com/pages/create.php**.

The first step is to choose a category. There are six main categories, each with subcategories, so think carefully about what best reflects your business. You can change these later by editing your page. Give your page a name – usually your business name, but think about which search terms people will use on Facebook to find you. Click **Get started** and start customising.

Like personal profiles, your page needs a profile picture (this can be your logo). With the timeline layout it is also important to include a large header image on your page (851 x 315 pixels). Your header image may also appear on the news feed of individuals whenever a friend of theirs likes your page – so make it eye-catching and something that communicates your brand. Don't include marketing text such as pricing or calls to action here though, as this is prohibited.

Your page needs a profile picture.

Click **Show** or **Hide** at the top right of your page to reveal or hide your **Admin Panel**. From this administrative area you can access detailed metrics for your page, see who has recently liked your page, and which items of content are the most popular. Also at the top of your page are drop-down menus called **Edit page** and **Build Audience**. From the **Edit page** menu you can edit your page, add other administrators and, importantly, change your 'voice' from your personal profile name to your page name. The drop-down option will switch between (in my case) **Use Facebook as Publishing Talk** and **Use Facebook as Jon Reed**. This enables you to choose which name you post under on your page – but also elsewhere on Facebook.

Frequently asked questions

How can I get my own Facebook URL?

Once you have 25 fans, you can claim your own 'vanity URL' instead of meaningless numbers. The Facebook page for this book is **www.facebook.com/ getuptospeed**, for example. Your URL doesn't necessarily have to match the name of your page, so think about search terms. You can then promote your page more easily to others with a memorable username that you can use on business cards, email signatures and elsewhere. Because Facebook also owns the domain fb.com and refers links on to facebook.com, Facebook URLs can be shortened to, e.g. **www.fb.com/getuptospeed** – which can be useful for sharing a link to your page on Twitter. Claim your username at **www.facebook.com/username**.

Customise your page

I won't lie to you – this is the technical part. If HTML scares you witless, feel free to skip this part or get someone else to do it for you. You can also just focus on your page updates for now and customise your page later on. But it will help if you at least have some understanding of what is possible with customised Facebook pages, if only so you can brief your web developer.

Customised Facebook pages are now the default way businesses use Facebook. Customising your header image is a good start, and an essential one – but we're really talking about custom 'tabs'.

What are tabs?

Facebook pages used to have navigation tabs, as found on many websites. This navigation feature has been replaced with a collection of rectangular boxes that sit below your header image and to the right of your short 'About' description. You might think of them as separate sections or pages within your page – but many people still call them tabs. Clicking on a tab will reveal a full-page view of its content. Your page content can be up to a maximum width of 810 pixels, and as long as you like.

By default, you already have two of these tabs on your page: Photos and Likes. Click the downward arrow next to these to reveal another four blank tabs, each with a '+' icon in their top-right-hand corner. You can add more than four tabs – new blank ones will appear as you create tabs. To add a new tab:

→ click the '+' icon to reveal a drop-down menu;

→ choose from a list of applications, including built-in Facebook apps such as Events and Notes, and any apps you have previously installed.

You can also move your tabs around. Once you have clicked the down arrow to reveal all your tabs, hovering over any existing tab will reveal a pencil icon in the top-right-hand corner. Click on this to reveal a drop-down menu that includes 'Swap position with:'. Use this to select the tab you want to switch with.

How to create custom tabs

Have you seen those 'Welcome' tabs and other bespoke tabs? What about those Facebook pages that invite you to 'like' the page to get access to additional content or downloads? Ever wondered how it's done? It's not as daunting as it looks.

Creating the content of your custom tabs is done with a technology called iFrames. This is a widely used way of embedding web pages or discrete bits of HTML within other web pages. There are a few Facebook apps that allow you to do this, and several third-party applications and services. Some third-party subscription services such as Wildfire or North Social provide templates to create pages, analytics and more, but can be expensive to maintain. There are free apps available within Facebook – do a search for the latest. These do change, but currently include:

→ **iFrame Apps – http://apps.facebook.com/iframe-apps**. Currently the cheapest and easiest option. Free, but extra options are available to premium members. To install, simply go to the app page and choose which page you want to add it to.

→ **Static HTML: iFrame tabs – http://apps.facebook.com/static_html_plus**. Another free application. To install it, go to the Facebook app page that's linked and click 'Add to My Page' on the right column.

Involver – www.involver.com/applications. Has a suite of Facebook applications and their iFrame app is called Static HTML. To install it, just go to the Involver website and click 'Install' next to the Static HTML app. Involver also allows fan-only content and you can add multiple custom tabs by clicking 'Add a Second Static HTML Application'.

Follow the instructions to install the apps on your page(s). Depending on which app you use, your content can be:

→ **HTML**. If you know some HTML, you can enter it directly into the window provided. I often use this method, but craft my code in the web design software Dreamweaver first, so that I can preview it and save it for future editing. If you don't know HTML, try copying and pasting some code, e.g. from your MailChimp email signup form or a page from your WordPress blog; hire someone to develop your pages (cheaper than the subscription options); or just plain ordinary text works too.

→ A **web page**. This is embedded as an iFrame. This gives you a lot of control over how your page looks, though you may need a web developer to design the pages you pull in.

→ An **image**. An easier option for the less technically-minded. A simple, powerful image that links to your website can be just as effective. Hire a graphic designer if necessary. And make it large: the full width of a Facebook page is 810 pixels.

→ A **fan gate**. 'Fan gating' means showing different content to fans and non-fans. Use this to incentivise 'likes' and tempt potential fans in with compelling content.

Your new tab shows up on your Facebook page (you may need to click the downwards-pointing arrow to reveal it). Hover over your tab, and click the pencil icon to reveal a menu. Click **Edit Settings** to change the title of your tab and to add a custom image for your tab. This must be 111 x 74 pixels (or larger – Facebook will resize). For example, I have a tab called 'Latest issue' on my Publishing Talk page, which has the top half of the latest magazine cover as its image.

Ways to use custom tabs

How will you use custom tabs? Think about what will communicate your brand and be valued by your community. Examples include:

→ **Welcome page**. While there is no longer a way to choose one of your tabs to be the first landing page people see, what you can do is create a tab on your top row that bears the words 'Start Here' or 'Welcome'.

→ **Use a fan gate**. Use fan gates to encourage 'likes' by offering an incentive such as a download – or simply access to a page with useful information or a video.

→ **Offer a download**. Author Tim Ferris offers a free chapter on his page at **www.facebook.com/TimFerriss**. Instead of using a fan gate, he uses one of several apps available from North Social called 'Exclusive'. This asks you to post a promotional message to your personal profile in exchange for the download – thus tapping into the viral nature of Facebook by promoting his book to your friends.

→ **Embed a video**. Provide some useful information for your community via video – and include an email signup box below your video with a prominent 'sign up for free for more information' button.

→ **Email signup**. iFrame Apps is one of the services that has an option to include a newsletter – albeit as a paid-for service. Or you could just copy and paste the email signup form code from MailChimp or other email service provider for free, or even use a simple link to your form. Making it easy for Facebook fans to subscribe to your newsletter will help you convert fans of your page to members of your email list.

→ **Pull in content**. Various apps will allow you to pull content into a Facebook tab, including YouTube videos and Flickr images. To pull in Instagram images, go to **http://statigr.am** and click the Promote tab.

→ **Contests**. Contests are becoming a way to increase engagement. They typically involve voting by the public and/or judging to determine the winner. While photo contests are common, other types include video entry, essay or caption. Some third-party services, including Wildfire, enable you to create contests, plus sweepstakes and quizzes.

Engage people with updates

Now that you have a page, you need some content. The way to add this is via status updates – just as you would with your personal profile. You can pay to promote your updates – but you won't need to if you keep your content relevant to your audience, consistent and engaging enough for them to want to like, comment on or share.

Content can be status updates, links, images, videos, offers, events, milestones or questions. Whether or not you use the built-in polls app, it is a good idea to ask questions of your fans some of the time to encourage discussion – for example, if you post a link to an opinion piece about a topic relevant to your industry. You can reply to comments on your page, and they appear indented in a discussion thread.

Use images where possible and appropriate, since the timeline layout gives weight to these. They take up more space in news feeds, so are seen more easily; and people are much more likely to engage with an image than a text-based update.

Use images where possible and appropriate.

By hovering over an individual post and clicking the down arrow to reveal a menu you can also:

→ **Highlight** it (star icon). This makes it the full width of your page.

→ **Hide** or **delete** it.

→ **Change its date** (clock icon).

→ **Pin** it (choose **Pin to Top**). This anchors your post to the top of your page for up to seven days, meaning it won't disappear down your timeline as you post new updates.

Promote your page

Whether or not you add custom tabs, one thing that is essential is to promote your page. Blog about it, tweet about it and include it in your email signature. But the most important place to do this is on your blog or website, by enabling people to 'like' your page directly from your site without even having to visit Facebook.

Create your **Facebook 'like' box** at **http://developers.facebook. com/docs/reference/plugins/like-box**. You can create a 'like' box for any Facebook page from here – just enter the URL of your page, and start customising. You can choose the dimensions, and whether or not to show profile images of some of your fans, or the 'stream' of latest activity. The most minimal option is simply to display your page's profile image, name and a 'like' button. Then simply add the code provided to your website, or paste it into a 'text' widget in your WordPress blog.

Another option is to promote your Facebook page on your blog or website with a 'badge' (**www.facebook.com/badges/page.php**). These are less interactive, but can include your latest status update. Finally, don't forget to include a Facebook icon in the collection of social media icons displayed prominently on your website.

Quick win

Promote your page with a social ad

'Social Ads' are what Facebook calls those ads you see on the right-hand side of your screen. They can be worth considering for a short period when you first launch something, to help raise awareness within your target audience, whether that's your website, a new product or service – or your new Facebook page.

They are also worth considering because they are highly targeted – not only by demographics such as gender, location and age, but by the keywords and job titles people include in their profiles. You can reach a small number of highly targeted individuals for very little cost.

You have the option of choosing pay per click, or pay per view. Because click-through rates on Facebook are so low, you should always choose pay per click. Like other PPC services, such as Google AdWords, you can set a budget limit, and spend as much or as little as you choose. Find out more at **www.facebook.com/advertising**.

Get Up to Speed with Online Marketing

Create a Facebook group

Pages are your main promotional tool on Facebook, but groups are also worth a mention. Groups can be useful for fostering a sense of community. They are useful if you want to encourage communication between group members, rather than broadcast your latest news and special offers to fans via your branded page. Think of pages as one-to-many and groups as many-to-many communication.

Groups can be open, closed or secret. My Publishing Talk group (**www.facebook.com/groups/publishingtalk**) is open, meaning anyone can see the group, who's in it and what they post. But you can also make a group closed, meaning only members can see posts; or secret, meaning only members can see the group. New members must be approved by an administrator or another member, depending on your settings; and you can if you wish set moderation controls so that an administrator must approve posts before they are added.

Create a Facebook event

Events are useful for product launches, conferences, training courses, seminars, etc., especially when many potential attendees are fans of your page or members of your group. Events can be created by:

1 Individuals/profiles – **www.facebook.com/events/create.php**.

2 Groups – click on the **Events** tab and then the **+ Create event** button.

3 Pages – click on your **Events** tab (create one if you need to), then the **+ Create event** button.

Manage the workload

You can cut down on time maintaining pages and groups by setting up multiple administrators to look after them. You can also use your page maintenance time more efficiently by scheduling updates in advance where possible. Use a social media dashboard such as HootSuite for this; or do it from within Facebook. One of the options at the bottom of your status update box is 'Schedule or backdate your post' – a little clock icon. You can add posts to your timeline in the past, such as your business milestones; or schedule a load of updates to publish at future dates.

Another important time-saver is aggregating your social media content so that an action you take elsewhere results in an automatic post to your Facebook page. There are three types of content you may want to push through to Facebook:

1 **Blogs**. Pull in your blog using Twitterfeed (**www.twitterfeed.com**). Twitterfeed links your blog's RSS feed to Twitter accounts – but also to Facebook. You can set up multiple feeds and send them to your profile, or to individual Facebook pages. You might even consider setting up a discrete RSS feed for a particular blog category and pushing just that content to a particular page, to keep it focused and relevant to your audience.

2 **Multimedia**. Enable other social media apps and services you use to automatically post to your page – where you consider the content to be appropriate to your Facebook audience. This is particularly useful for any content you create, such as photographs, video or audio. You could also use Facebook applications on some of your tabs that pull in content, such as Flickr or Instagram photos, or YouTube videos.

3 **Updates**. You can link Facebook to Twitter so that your tweets become your Facebook page status update. Use this with caution, though, as not every tweet may be relevant to your Facebook audience, and could annoy fans. Consider the Selective Tweets app (**http://apps.facebook.com/selectivetwitter**) so that only tweets ending in #fb go to your page. This works with multiple Twitter accounts and pages.

A mix of these automatic updates, plus pre-scheduled updates, should keep enough content coming onto your page to engage fans while freeing you up for other tasks.

Measure your results

With groups, you have little more than the number of members to go on. For Social Ads, you get the sort of statistics you would expect:

impressions, click-through rates, traffic and costs. You should record these for each campaign you run, to get an idea of which are the most effective. But it is with pages that Facebook metrics really come into their own, and this is a key reason for using pages in the first place.

The most obvious measure of your success is your number of fans. Fans are important because they have potential to see your updates in their news feed. But this is a fairly blunt measure. A more important measure is the level of engagement fans have with your page. Engagement here is defined as clicking anywhere in a post, including liking, commenting and sharing your content.

To access your stats, click **Show** at the top right of your page to reveal your **Admin Panel**. Click **See All** next to the Insights graph towards the bottom. The summary figures at the top show:

→ **Total Likes** – how many people like your page.

→ **Friends of Fans** – number of fans plus all their friends.

→ **People Talking About This** – the number of people who have 'created a story' about your page. In Facebook terms, this means people who have liked, posted or shared your page or page content.

→ **Weekly Total Reach** – people who have seen any content associated with your page, including ads or sponsored stories.

Below the graph, there are detailed insights for every page post, which relate to the first 28 days after posting. You can click on the numbers given for the first three metrics for further breakdown:

→ **Reach** – the number of unique people who saw your post.

→ **Engaged users** – how many clicked on your post.

→ **Talking about this** – the number of likes, comments and shares.

→ **Virality** – the percentage of unique people who saw your post who 'created a story' about it.

These metrics are all available on the **Overview** page view, which is selected by default. There are additional links next to this at the top of your Insights page: **Likes**, **Reach** and **Talking about this**, all of which give you detailed demographic information about your fans. Likes is the most useful here. The information about your fans can be useful for market research, developing new products or services, or just gaining a better understanding of who your customers are. It includes demographic breakdown by age, gender, geographic location and language.

Aside from your Insights page, you can also see how many people saw a particular post by looking at the link underneath it, which will say something like '461 people saw this post'. Hovering over this will break it down by organic and viral; and show you a link to stats for your most popular post (e.g. '2,065 people saw your most popular post'), which can act as a benchmark of what you can achieve. Use these metrics to assess which types of post work best with your audience.

Another way to find out which posts work best for you is to split-test your posts – though you can only do this when you have over 5,000 fans. Once you do, you should see an additional 'target' icon below your status box. Click this to make your post visible only to a particular segment of your fans. This in itself is useful simply to keep content relevant when you have a lot of fans; but you can also use it to test which posts are the most effective. Try this approach with, say, different images or different calls to action. Or use the same post targeted at different groups to see which are the most responsive or have the highest conversion rate.

Facebook best practice

1 **Claim your username**. Get up to 25 fans as soon as you can, to claim your Facebook username.

2 **Include images** on your page – especially a header image, but post pictures on your timeline too.

3 **Keep content fresh**. Alternate between images, links, videos and simple status updates or polls. Ask questions, and be responsive. Post fairly often – you are likely only to have a window of a few hours when your content is visible in timelines before it is buried by new stories.

4 **Pull in your blog** to automate the process and keep a flow of regular valuable content.

5 **Pre-schedule updates** using HootSuite or from within Facebook. Scheduling will create consistency in your posting.

6 **Customise your page** with bespoke 'tabs'. Use these to share more information about your business, showcase products, incentivise email signups, pull in content, run contests and specific promotions.

7 **Promote your page** using a 'like' box on your blog or website.

8 **Use groups** to build a professional network, or a support community for customers and clients.

9 **Use ads** when you launch a new page, product, service or business – they are useful for raising awareness.

10 **Analyse your metrics** to keep your page content relevant and compelling. Split-test your posts once you have over 5,000 fans.

Take action

→ **Set up** a personal profile if you don't yet have one.

→ **Create and customise** a page for your business.

→ **Promote** your page with a 'like' box on your blog and a Social Ad on Facebook.

→ **Create** a group to facilitate discussion and networking.

Develop leads on LinkedIn

How to take your business networking online

Chapter Twelve

With over 225 million users in over 200 countries, LinkedIn is the world's largest professional social network. It may be smaller than the mighty Facebook or Twitter. But it has a particular niche focus: professional networking. Where Facebook users have friends and Twitter users have followers, LinkedIn users have contacts. Use it to develop business contacts, or to develop sales leads, particularly if you sell to other businesses.

What is LinkedIn?

Initially little more than a place to keep an online version of your CV or résumé and make business connections – a bit like handing out business cards in cyberspace – LinkedIn has evolved into a more social tool. It has features such as groups and company pages, similar to features you might use on Facebook or Google+ – but they are tailored to a business and professional audience. LinkedIn is worth a look even if you just set up a profile then ignore it, since it's another place for people to find you. But you may be surprised by its marketing potential, particularly for business-to-business (B2B) marketing. LinkedIn has been slimmed down and simplified lately and the three main services that you will use are:

1 **Profile**. Your online CV or résumé – important for building trust and connections on LinkedIn. LinkedIn is an even more closed network than Facebook, and you can only send connection invitations to people you know, have some business connection with, whose email address you know, or who you have been introduced to via a mutual contact.

2 **Company pages**. Similar to business pages on Facebook or Google+, these allow you to present your brand and promote your business.

3 **Groups**. Groups are great for building a large following around a niche topic and can be a great way to engage your community with useful content – and build up a mailing list.

 You may be surprised by its marketing potential.

There are five main navigation links:

1 **Home** – similar to Facebook, this is your news feed of updates, links and activity from your network. You can also post status updates from here, which can be made visible to everyone or just shared with your connections. Updates can be liked, commented on and shared.

2 **Profile** – your personal profile or online CV/résumé – which can also be edited from this page.

3 **Network** – the main **Network** link (or its **Contacts** sub-menu link) can be used to view and organise your network. You can also send messages to discrete segments of your network, which can be a powerful tool.

4 **Jobs** – search for jobs or post jobs (a paid-for service).

5 **Interests** – click the **Companies** drop-down link to see the company pages you follow or manage your own. Use the **Groups** drop-down link to see groups you are a member of or to create a new one. You can also follow **Influencers** from here.

Why LinkedIn works for business

LinkedIn has a valuable demographic for marketers – and an older one. Seventy-nine per cent of its members are over 35, and their average age is 44. This is unsurprising for a professional network. Its members tend to be senior, affluent, influential, open for business – and open to doing business with you online. Although you should avoid anything spammy or off-topic, marketing messages are less frowned upon on LinkedIn. It is a business network, after all – so promoting your business on it is fine. Just keep it relevant to the people you're talking to.

LinkedIn works for business in several ways.

Building business connections

Whether it's getting back in touch with old colleagues or meeting new contacts, LinkedIn is like a big business networking party where everyone is handing out business cards, and saying 'You must meet my colleague X' or 'I'm looking for a graphic designer, can you recommend someone?' Use it to tell people what you do, but also for introductions and recruitment. In addition it is a useful way to make connections with key decision makers at organisations you want to work with. LinkedIn shows you your number of contacts – but, unlike Facebook, also calculates a number of potential contacts in your wider network of friends of friends. This is a powerful database of professionals who are likely to be within your broad areas of interest, who you are not directly connected to, but to whom you could get an introduction via people you do know. This is like real-life business networking, except that you can see which people your business contacts know in front of you on your screen, and decide who you think might be useful for you to know.

 LinkedIn is like a big business networking party where everyone is handing out business cards.

Positioning yourself as an expert

Share information about your area of expertise, whether via your profile, company page, professional groups you are a member of, or your own group. The core of a LinkedIn group is the discussion area: use this to share knowledge and position yourself as an expert.

Promoting your business

You can promote your business with adverts, though these can become expensive. The two best tools to promote your business on LinkedIn are free: company pages and groups. Use company pages to promote your brand and make connections. People can 'follow' company pages and receive your 'Company Updates', as well as use them to learn more about your company, your products and services, and your job opportunities. Groups are useful as topic-based communities. Join groups in your area of interest, and post relevant messages to them. Then create your own to engage your community of interest with useful information, and build a 'list' of members. We will look at company pages and groups in more detail next.

Get Up to Speed with Online Marketing

Frequently asked questions

How can I use LinkedIn for recruitment?

If you want to hire someone, your professional network is an excellent starting point, and you can mention that you are looking for staff in a status update. LinkedIn has also had jobs boards on Groups for a while now; and you can announce that you are looking for staff via an ad. But if you're particularly interested in using LinkedIn for recruitment it now includes a (paid-for) suite of tools to help you go beyond your personal network to recruit from across LinkedIn and promote your brand to potential employees. This includes highlighting your employees and posting jobs that target the right candidates using automated job matching. See LinkedIn Talent Solutions for more information (**http://talent.linkedin.com**).

LinkedIn in action

How a China-based import/export agent built a $5m business with LinkedIn

JMF International Trade Group Ltd (**www.jmftradegroup.com**) is an international import/export agency run by Hong-Kong-based James Filbird. He built the company to $5 million in revenue, and attributes this largely to his efforts on LinkedIn (**www.linkedin.com/in/globaltrading**) – the only major social network not blocked by the Chinese government.

When LinkedIn hit 100 million members, James was highlighted as one of 100 success stories: people who used the platform particularly well. Developing 'an outstanding profile' is something he sees as the foundation for success on LinkedIn. He recommends updating your profile every other day with a quote, link or news. When people like or comment on your updates, other people can see that, and it helps spread the word.

But James sees groups as the biggest resource on LinkedIn. 'Groups are where I go digging for gold,' he says. Getting involved in group discussions, and creating his own discussions, is the main way he has built up his network – and business – on LinkedIn. Used well, groups help you 'become a thought-leader, an influencer, and a magnet for the type of people you are looking for'.

▶

When making new connections it pays to be choosy. It's not about the number but the quality of connections you develop on LinkedIn. James targets the inventor community, who often need help with prototyping, product development, manufacturing and packaging. He finds groups to join by searching for keywords in the 'groups search' function, seeing which groups his connections are in, and receiving group recommendations from his connections. He recommends joining the maximum 50 groups allowable, getting daily email digests for 5–10 groups, spending at least an hour a week participating in discussions, sending connection invitations to people you meet in discussions – and taking things offline by asking connections if they would like to connect by phone or Skype. Business is all about relationships, after all – and LinkedIn is a powerful, professional relationship-building tool.

Get the idea: Start by building a great profile on LinkedIn, and update your status regularly. Use LinkedIn groups as a way of building new contacts in your field – but think quality rather than quantity. Offer solutions rather than just marketing messages, to position yourself as a thought-leader. Join the maximum allowable number of groups, but research which ones are worth joining, and limit the number of email digests to a manageable number. Think about who your audience is, get active, create discussions, comments and likes – and use LinkedIn to build your personal brand.

Get up to speed with LinkedIn

In this section, we will look at the steps you need to take to get up to speed with LinkedIn.

→ Optimise your profile.
→ Set up your company page.
→ Create a LinkedIn Group.

Optimise your profile

In order to use the promotional features of LinkedIn effectively, you must have a good profile. This is the foundation of LinkedIn, which is built around trusted contacts. Specifically, if you want to set up a company page, one of the pre-requisites is to have a 'profile strength' that is listed as 'Intermediate' or 'All Star'. That means you need a fairly complete and detailed profile.

Think of your LinkedIn profile as selling copy. On Facebook you might talk about your hobbies or family in your personal profile. For LinkedIn, imagine you are updating your CV or résumé, or writing down your elevator pitch. Focus on your career history, education, achievements and what you can offer your contacts through your business. Add links to your websites so that people can find more information, and use plenty of keywords relevant to your industry, to boost your search results. Your latest activity shows at the top of your profile – but you can drag and drop the other 'boxes' of information around, so make sure you have your most important higher up. This will probably be your summary, but you might also want your experience, publications or projects high up too.

Build your network by importing your email contacts and searching for your business contacts. Look at your contacts' connections too for anyone you know. LinkedIn will also suggest people to connect to, based on your network, and is remarkably good at finding people for you – I'm still often surprised at how often LinkedIn correctly guesses 'people you may know'. This is partly due to the restrictions built into the system. You are discouraged from connecting with just *anyone*.

LinkedIn will also suggest people to connect to.

One part of your profile is 'Recommendations' – short testimonials written by contacts with whom you have done business. These are equivalent to references you may include with your CV or résumé, and don't be afraid to ask for them. There's even a form to make it easy for you. Go to **www.linkedin.com/recRequests**. This can also be a useful way to add testimonials to your website, since you can ask if you can quote from their recommendation on your website too. People can also endorse the skills and experience on your profile with a few simple checks.

Bear in mind at all times that your audience on LinkedIn may be subtly different from your audience on Facebook or Twitter. With all social networks, keep your status updates and postings relevant to your community of interest and the network you're communicating on.

Set up your company page

A company page is a place where you can build a following and showcase products and services. Any LinkedIn member can follow a company that has set up a company page to get 'Company Updates'. Because you can list individual products and services and provide a lot of information about each, company pages are also an opportunity for LinkedIn members to research your products and services. You can add a new company page if you meet all of the following requirements:

→ You're a current company employee and your position is listed in the 'Experience' section on your profile.

→ You have a company email address added and confirmed on your LinkedIn account – and your company's email domain is unique to the company (i.e. not Gmail, etc.).

→ You have several connections and your profile strength is listed as 'Intermediate' or 'All Star'.

Then select **Companies** from the **Interests** menu on the homepage and look for the name of your company. Click **Edit** at the top right of the Company Overview tab. If the Edit link is not visible, do the following to ensure that your profile is properly connected to the company name:

1 Click **Profile** at the top of your homepage.

2 Click **Edit** next to the position in the Experience section of your profile.

3 Click on **Change Company** and begin typing the name of the company.

4 A drop-down menu appears. Click the correct name of the company and click **Update**.

If you are still unable to edit information on your LinkedIn company page, you can contact Customer Service with your company name. Make sure you have an email address of the company registered to your account.

Company pages, like most social networks now, have a greater emphasis on visual content. So your first step in creating your page is to add a profile image (this could be your logo) and a header image (646 x 220 pixels).

Your company page has three navigation links at the top:

1 **Home** – this includes your summary or 'About us' blurb and company information. Consider this your elevator pitch. Include keywords to facilitate searches, and make sure you add some 'Company Specialities'. The 'Products' section in the sidebar is particularly useful, as it also shows the names, details and profile images of people who have recommended specific products and services on your page – a good reason to try to solicit these! Recommendations are key to sales success with social media.

2 **Products** – your products and services, each with an individual listing complete with a 100 x 80 pixel image, blurb, features and benefits, links to contacts who can provide more information, any special offer details – even an embedded YouTube product video if you have one. Best of all, it includes a specific weblink for each product or service – essential for driving traffic to your website, and driving sales.

3 **Insights** – a detailed demographic breakdown of your followers and company page visitors. See the 'Measure your results section' for more on this.

If you are using LinkedIn Talent Solutions, you get a fourth link too – **Careers**. This showcases employees, information about your company culture, and latest jobs alongside 'Company Updates'. Take a look at Google's careers page for an example of this in action: **www.linkedin. com/company/google/careers**. However, this is a paid-for service, and likely only to be of interest to larger organisations. If you are a small business or entrepreneur, find a cheaper way to recruit.

Seven benefits of company pages

1 **Brand awareness**. If you have employees, it's likely that they will list their employer (you) on their LinkedIn profiles. Anyone who connects with their profile may also click on the link to their employer – which will take them straight to your company page.

2 **Product awareness**. You can talk about what your business has to offer in a general sense on your company page – but you can also

list discrete products and services. Visitors can see your products and services – and can also see how many of their connections have recommended them.

3 **Search engine visibility**. LinkedIn has its own search facility for finding companies and jobs, but these will also show up in search engine results.

4 **Follower engagement**. Company pages allow status updates, known as 'Company Updates' – these can include images, video, presentations – and any sort of file. Followers can like, comment on or share your updates – just like Facebook. You can choose to share your status with **All followers** or **Targeted audience**. This is a bit like the status targeting function on Facebook pages – except that you don't need 5,000 followers first.

5 **Lead generation**. Status updates and content sharing, particularly when coupled with a compelling call to action, result in traffic being driven to your website. Use this to generate leads.

6 **Recommendations**. Customers can add recommendations, which appear prominently on your page. This adds credibility to your offering by showing authentic endorsement from trusted followers and connections.

7 **Market research**. Followers of your company page are likely to be among your strongest advocates and interested in what you do next. Use your 'Company Updates' to share information about forthcoming products – and invite them to contribute to their development.

Create a LinkedIn Group

LinkedIn groups are communities of interest within the wider LinkedIn network. Many professional associations have LinkedIn groups, which are worth joining and contributing to. But with well over a million LinkedIn groups to choose from, there are bound to be several relevant to you. One of the advantages of groups is that they can help you grow your personal network within those niches that interest you most, since you can invite members from your group to become contacts.

You can also set up your own in your area of interest. Search existing groups first to see where the opportunities are to differentiate yourself. Groups tend to work best as topic-based forums or professional networks. For example, I have a Publishing Talk group that I use to promote the website and connect with publishing professionals around the world. LinkedIn groups are great for engaging a more professional, business-orientated segment of your market. For me, this makes it a sensible place to promote the social media workshops I offer to publishers, since people on LinkedIn tend to be interested in professional development. Think about what aspect of your offering might fit this sort of professional profile.

You can also create subgroups. For example, the Small Biz Nation group (**http://www.linkedin.com/groups?gid=2885246**) is a collaboration between Intel and HP providing a LinkedIn community for business owners and marketers. It has around 20,000 members and a subgroup called 'Special Offers from HP & Intel' with around 750 members. That is smart marketing, as those members of the main group have identified themselves as being open to offers.

To create your LinkedIn group, select **Groups** from the **Interests** drop-down menu at the top of your screen, click **Create a Group** and fill in the details.

Make sure you upload a logo – once people start joining, this 'badge' will show up on their profile, and if your group looks interesting to their contacts, they may click on it and join too. Add a description with plenty of keywords, include your website, and choose a group type. This will most likely be 'Networking Group' or 'Professional Group'.

You have the option of choosing either:

→ **Open Access** – any LinkedIn member may join this group without requiring approval from a manager.

→ **Request to Join** – users must request to join this group and be approved by a manager.

You should generally choose the former to reduce any barriers to building up your membership. Once you have your group set up, you'll need to add content to it to keep people interested. Group members can start discussions, add news, and post job ads in your group (subject to the settings you choose), but you need to do some of the work too. Things you can add are:

- → **Discussions** – start a discussion topic, or simply post a message to the discussion area. As administrator, you can also make this a 'featured' item that appears at the top of the list.
- → **Links** – attach links to discussions, with a short description.
- → **Polls** – within the discussion area you can start a discussion or a poll. Ask a question, and specify up to five multiple choice answers. This can be useful to engage your members, and for bits of ad-hoc market research.
- → **Job Ads** – your group comes with a jobs board, which you can choose to use or not.

Add at least some content before inviting your contacts, even if it is just a welcome message. And don't invite everyone – just those who you think will be interested. Promote your group as you would with a Facebook group or any new social media channel you start using: put it in your email signature, include a prominent link on your website, write a blog post about it, mention it in your next email newsletter, tweet about it, etc.

Don't invite everyone – just those who you think will be interested.

A significant benefit of groups – whether your own or someone else's that you post to – is that the items you submit to them are included in digest emails to group members who accept notifications from the group. With your own group, you can also **Send an Announcement** to all the members of your group, which sends an email as well as posting to the discussion area. Use this sparingly (LinkedIn will only allow one of these per week) and think carefully about your message content, as you would with any other mass mailing. Because these emails come from linkedin.com, they have a high deliverability – they're less likely to get caught in spam filters.

Use a LinkedIn social bookmarking button to share your posts

LinkedIn no longer allows you to pull your latest blog posts into the discussion area of your group automatically – nor to post to multiple groups from the status update box on your Home or Profile page. However, rather than manually adding links to multiple places, you can save time by using a LinkedIn social bookmarking button on your own blog.

→ Use a WordPress plugin such as Shareaholic to add social bookmarking buttons to the end of all your blog posts. Make sure LinkedIn is one of them.

→ Click the **Add to LinkedIn** button below a post you want to share.

→ A new window opens, allowing you to choose to post the link to your profile (with a status update if you wish), to groups and/or to individuals.

→ Check the groups box and start typing the name of your own group – plus any other groups that you are a member of that you want to share your post with.

→ Click the blue **Share** button at the bottom.

This makes it easy to share your content as a status update on your profile, but also post it to groups. Use it wisely though, and don't spam multiple groups with off-topic content!

Manage the workload

Manage your contacts

If you use LinkedIn primarily for its original purpose – networking and building contacts – this can become harder to manage as the size of your network increases. A tool called Five Hundred Plus (**www. fivehundredplus.com**) can help you do this more efficiently. This is a personal 'Customer relationship management' (CRM) app that helps you cultivate your most valuable connections and always remember what you said to them last time you were in touch. It also includes a handy dashboard in which you can view all your contacts – and drag them into columns showing how often you think you should contact them, e.g. weekly, monthly, quarterly or yearly.

Post your blog automatically

Although you can no longer import RSS feeds into your groups, you can post your blog automatically to your profile using Twitterfeed. This includes the title and description from your feed and lets LinkedIn pick the most relevant thumbnail image. If you prefer, you can set up the service so that it always posts the same static image with your updates – just specify an image URL.

Schedule updates

Keep your LinkedIn status updates fresh and use your time efficiently by pre-scheduling your updates. Use HootSuite to manage updates for your profile, your company pages and your groups – plus any group that you are a member of. You can only link to five social media accounts on the free version, so you will need to upgrade to HootSuite Pro if you want to post to a lot of groups in this way.

Appoint multiple managers

Spread the workload of managing your company pages and groups by adding extra people. You can add multiple administrators on company pages so long as you are connected to them on LinkedIn. On groups, you can promote up to nine members to manager status, and up to 50 to moderator. Click on the **Manage** tab, select **Participants** from the left-hand menu and then the **Members** tab. Below each member profile there is a link to **Change Role** (to Manager or Moderator).

Measure your results

Your LinkedIn profile has some basic numbers relating to connections and views. But the important metrics are the detailed data available for your groups and pages.

Company pages

Company pages come with the following metrics built in:

→ **Follower Insights** shows how people are engaging with your updates, and a bar chart of follower demographics broken down by company size, seniority, industry function and geographic region.

→ **Page Insights** provides a bar chart about page visitor demographics, and two graphs for page views and unique visitors, both of which can be views for All, Overview or Products & Services. In addition it shows how many clicks you've received on your Products & Services page.

→ **Employee Insights** is a useful page for larger organisations, to keep track of new employees and where they worked previously, who has been promoted or left recently, top skills and expertise, and who has received the most recommendations.

In addition, very much like Facebook posts, you also get information about individual items you post as 'Company Updates'. Twenty-four hours after you post, you will see some metrics underneath your post, including the number of impressions, clicks, shares – and a percentage score for engagement. Underneath this you will also see the number of likes, comments and shares displayed in brackets next to the like, comment and share links.

Finally, use tracking links or unique landing pages on your 'Product' page if you want to measure the referral traffic coming from your company page. Because you can use specific URLs for each product or service, you can measure results for each one you list.

Groups

LinkedIn groups have detailed demographic information on your members, plus information on member growth and activity. Go to the **More...** tab in your group and choose **Group Statistics**. Demographics include Seniority, Function, Location and Industry. They are available not just to you as a group manager, but to anyone who is a member of a group – so you can also look at your competitors'.

LinkedIn best practice

1 **Keep your content professional, businesslike, and regular**. Manage your updates to profiles, company pages and groups (your own and others you are a member of) with HootSuite, and post your blog to your profile using Twitterfeed.

2 **Share blog posts** from your blog via a LinkedIn social bookmarking button.

3 Use **company pages** to build brand awareness, promote products and services and drive sales leads.

4 **Create multiple variations of your products page**. LinkedIn can target your 'Products' page to different segments, and serve different versions to different audiences based on their profile content. This might simply be a geographic split, such as different versions of the same product targeted at the US or Europe. Create a **Default** version, then click **New Audience** below it, give your market segment a name, select your targeting criteria and save it.

5 **Include banners on your 'Products' page**. You can include up to three rotating banners on this page (640 x 220 pixels), each of which can link to a specific web address.

6 **Feature** up to five products on your 'Products' page. This is useful if you have a lot of products, and you want to keep your bestsellers or most important products and services easy to find.

7 Use **LinkedIn Talent Solutions** for recruitment – if you can afford it!

8 Use **groups** to build a professional network around a topic area. Start and contribute to discussions, and use the 'Send an Announcement' feature to contact members by email.

9 **Set 'Group Rules'** and use moderation controls for your group to avoid spam links being emailed to your members.

10 **Consider LinkedIn ads** to promote your new company page or group (**see http://linkedin.com/ads**) – but use them sparingly as they can be expensive.

Take action

→ **Optimise** your profile. Keep it business-focused, add connections and solicit recommendations.

→ **Pull** your blog into your profile using Twitterfeed.

→ **Set up** your company page and list your products and services.

→ **Join** groups relevant to your business and contribute to some discussions – then start your own.

Tap into Twitter

How to use the real-time web to build a following

Chapter Thirteen

Twitter isn't about sharing what you had for lunch. There are smart, informed, creative people being witty on Twitter in 140 characters or fewer. These people also take an interest in the world, current events and topics that interest them. And they recommend and buy stuff – and businesses as well as individuals can have Twitter accounts. According to HubSpot, 42 per cent of companies have acquired a customer via Twitter. This chapter looks at how you can be in that 42 per cent and use Twitter effectively to get your message across.

What is Twitter?

News feeds and status updates are common features to most social networks now. Twitter is essentially *only* these two features, combined into an ever-updating timeline. A short update, or 'tweet', tells the world what you're up to. That can seem a bit pointless when you first join, or to be a bit like a cocktail party where everyone already knows each other and speaks in a strange shorthand. But as you get into Twitter, a whole world of possibilities opens up.

As you get into Twitter, a whole world of possibilities opens up.

As well as short updates, you can share links, images and video. Twitter is great for sharing links, which makes it a brilliant outreach tool for most forms of social media content – especially blogs.

On Twitter, instead of friends, fans or connections, people have followers. Anyone can follow any Twitter account they like *unless* tweets are 'protected', meaning follow requests must be approved – rarely done, and not a good idea unless you want to be invisible! People you follow can see that you have followed them – but may or may not follow you back. They can also see every time you mention their username with an @ sign in front of it, e.g. @jonreed.

There are four main views available. The navigation links at the top left of your screen are:

→ **Home** – the latest tweets from everyone you follow.

→ **Connect** – your 'Interactions' – i.e. whenever anyone includes your @username, retweets or favorites your tweet, follows you or adds you to a list, that action will show up here.

→ **Discover** – a little more like a Facebook news feed, this shows a timeline of recent tweets tailored to what Twitter thinks you will be interested in.

→ **Me** – your profile page, showing your biography and the latest tweets you have posted. This is what people see when they visit your Twitter account. This also displays a count of how many tweets you have posted, how many people you follow and how many followers you have.

Next to this is a search box, and a cog wheel icon which includes the drop-down menu options **Edit profile**, **Direct messages**, **Lists** and **Settings**. Direct messages (DM) are private messages and can be sent to anyone who follows you. Lists are useful for creating a discrete list of people on Twitter whose tweets you want to view in a separate timeline. You can also sign out of your account from here, and sign into another account. Finally, at the right-hand side of the top bar is a blue button with a quill pen icon. Click this to write a new tweet. There are two icons below your text window: a camera (to upload an image) and a map pin (to add your location).

There are additional links on each individual tweet. To the right of a tweet you will see a date stamp, e.g. '2h' or '1 Apr'. This shows when the tweet was posted. Click on it to see the tweet on a separate web page, with further information below it such as how many people have retweeted or favourited it. You can also see this information by clicking on an 'Expand' link, which you may see below a tweet.

Other links below a tweet may include 'View conversation', 'View summary', 'View photo' or 'View video'. But it's the links that only become visible when you hover over a tweet that you will use most:

1 **Reply** – send a reply that starts with @username. This is visible to anyone who visits your profile and in the timelines of anyone who follows both you and the person you are replying to. Mentions, by contrast, are used to mean a mention of someone's @username within a tweet (rather than at the very start), and are more visible.

2 **Retweet** – pass a tweet on to your followers. Visible on your profile page and in the timelines of people who follow you. Displays the profile picture and name of the original tweeter, with 'Retweeted by [Your Name]' underneath. You can also 'manually' retweet by tweeting 'RT @username:' followed by a cut-and-pasted tweet; or even 'MT @username' to mean 'modified tweet' if you paraphrase it.

3 **Favorite** – add a tweet to your list of favourites. Other people can see these by clicking 'Favorites' on your profile. This can be a useful place to save any client testimonials or positive customer feedback.

4 **More** – less often used, but it can be useful to 'Email Tweet' to someone or 'Embed Tweet' on your blog or website with a bit of code provided.

Also on the left-hand sidebar you will find:

→ **Media** – on your profile page only, a collection of thumbnail images of images you have uploaded and videos you have shared.

→ **Who to Follow** – suggestions based on the people you follow already – and who they follow.

→ **Trending topics** – the 10 most commonly-used words or phrases being used on Twitter right now. These may or may not be hashtags, and can be viewed as global trends or narrowed down geographically.

Why does Twitter work for business?

The value of Twitter is in its ability to reach a vast yet niche audience of people who are interested in what you have to say – and wherever they are. The real-time 'breaking news' aspect of Twitter, coupled with its widespread use on smartphones makes it a powerful medium for providing valuable information for your community of interest where and when they want it – and being responsive to trends, events and customer feedback. About half the people on Twitter use it from their phones.

Twitter's usefulness to you as a business is similar to building an email list – and it is an opt-in list, since people have sought you out and chosen to follow you for the valuable, interesting content you provide.

For people who follow you, your usefulness will depend on the content you tweet. This should focus on information that is of interest to your niche and relevant links to your blog posts to drive traffic, but can also include time-limited discount codes. According to a 2011 survey by Compete, 94 per cent of Twitter users follow brands for 'discounts and promos', and 88 per cent for 'free stuff'. These are both things you can share on Twitter.

Don't be afraid to show a little personality.

However, don't be afraid to show a little personality: 87 per cent also said they followed brands for 'fun and entertainment'. Tone of voice is important on Twitter. You don't need to be as businesslike as you do on LinkedIn, for example. Keep it informal, and personable, even entertaining – but relevant, responsive and helpful too. Above all, be yourself. Tweet links and information that serve your community, keep it authentic and informal, and your followers, brand awareness and website traffic will increase.

Twitter in action

How an Indian beer brand spreads word of mouth with tweetups

Kingfisher Beer (**www.kingfisherworld.com**) is a well-known Indian beer brand. They have over 30,000 Twitter followers at @kingfisherworld, and engage them with regular tweetups (meet-ups in real life). They call these 'BeerUps', supply free beer, and use the hashtag #KFBeerUp to promote them.

The tweetups take place every Saturday in a different Indian city, and are announced a month in advance on their website and on Twitter. Anyone who uses Twitter can come along, though the guest list is restricted to the first 50–80 people to register with Twtvite, a free tool that Kingfisher uses to manage invitations (**http://twtvite.com**). Places fill up quickly. Having announced a Jaipur #KFBeerUp in April 2013, @kingfisher world tweeted: 'Hyderabad took 16 minutes to fill up all the #KFBeerUp slots. Jaipur beer-heads, think you can RSVP faster than Hyderabad? #KFBeerlympics'.

The events themselves are sometimes recorded and put on YouTube: a 2012 Mumbai event hosted by stand-up comedian Rohan Joshi and featuring local band Tough on Tobacco can be seen at **www.youtube.com/watch?v=Ogs_Ihz43y0**. This helps promote events by giving a flavour of previous ones, and the Kingfisher logo and '@kingfisherworld' appears on-screen throughout to encourage follows. Kingfisher has its own channel at **www.youtube.com/user/KingofGoodTimes**.

From the time Kingfisher announces a new event, word spreads on Twitter: people invite their friends using @usernames and Twitter starts buzzing with hashtag #KFBeerUp. The events help spread word of mouth during and after events too, as people tweet about them and share their own photos and videos, reaching thousands with the #KFBeerUp hashtag. Although events may be restricted to as few as 50 people, they promote brand loyalty among those who attend and brand enthusiasm among the wider Twitter community – all of which leads to increased sales in the future.

Get the idea: Engage your community with regular tweetups and give away some free sample products to get people talking about them on Twitter. Use a unique hashtag, create a positive experience, and film an event to promote future ones. Retweet positive tweets about your brand that result from your tweetup. You don't have to be a big beer brand to offer some free drinks, nor do you need to book comedians or bands. Just book a function room or an area of a bar and manage the whole process with Twtvite.

Get up to speed with Twitter

In this section we'll look at the essential steps you need to take to use Twitter effectively for your business.

→ Create your Twitter account.

→ Start a useful news feed.

→ Build your followers.

→ Engage your audience.

Create your Twitter account

First of all you need to go to **http://twitter.com** and create an account if you don't yet have one. You can create more than one account – such as a personal account and a business one – so long as you use a different email address to register each.

1 **Choose a username**. You can change your 'Full name' and username later if you want – but think carefully about the username you choose, since this will appear in the URL (e.g. **http://twitter.com/jonreed**). It's a bit like registering a web address.

2 **Upload a profile picture**. You must have one of these. If you stick with the default egg icon you will not be taken seriously on Twitter and it will be hard to attract followers.

3 **Add a biography and web address**. Add a 160-character biography. This can be a personal biography or a description of your business. Biographies can include links – including hashtags and @usernames. Your web address appears below this, alongside your location.

4 **Add a header image**. Like many other networks, Twitter now has header images on profiles. Go to **Settings** and **Profile** to add yours (1252 x 626 pixels). This is another opportunity to communicate your brand in a visual way.

5 **Customise your design**. Go to **Settings**, click on **Design** and choose colours that match your branding. You can choose a bespoke background image if you like, and this is a good idea to reinforce your brand.

Frequently asked questions

What are hashtags?

Hashtags are simply clickable keywords. Put the # symbol immediately before a word or phrase (with no spaces or punctuation) and it becomes a link. When someone clicks on a hashtag, it will link through to a new timeline made up of everyone who has included that hashtag in their tweets. Hashtags are often used to play word games, or to discuss and follow an event in real time, such as a television show or a conference. It may sound frivolous, but one of the best ways ▶

to get to grips with hashtags and how they are used it is to watch your favourite TV show and live-tweet it. This simply means watching TV while tweeting about the show, making sure to include the hashtag in your tweets. Follow the discussion on Twitter on a hashtag timeline page, or by using an app such as Twitterfall (**http://twitterfall.com**). Hashtags have also caught on with other networks: they can also be used in Pinterest, Google+ and Instagram – and now even Facebook.

Start a useful news feed

The best way to build up a large following of people who are interested in your particular niche is to set up a topic-based business account to tweet links, tips, blog posts and information relevant to your community of interest. You can then build a loyal following as an authentic, trusted voice in your field. This will make people want to follow you, build an opted-in list for you, and draw them on to your website. As with any form of social media, it's the usefulness of your content that will attract followers.

 Build a loyal following as an authentic, trusted voice in your field.

Here are the top things you should tweet to create a useful news feed. Some of these can be set up to tweet automatically, saving you time while keeping your audience engaged:

1 **Relevant links**. Tweets are most useful when they include a relevant link to something useful or interesting. Although Twitter will shorten links for you, to make the most of your 140 characters, the URL shortening service Bitly (**http://bitly.com**) is useful because you can use it with multiple Twitter accounts and it comes with metrics on click-throughs.

2 **Your blog**. The best way of generating web traffic based on relevant, contextual links is to tweet your blog. You can set up an account with Twitterfeed (**www.twitterfeed.com**) to link any

blog to a Twitter account. Whenever you publish a new post, it will automatically tweet to your account with a link back to your blog post. You can also set up a separate Twitterfeed to tweet the *comments* RSS feed from your blog too. This keeps the conversation going – and the traffic coming.

3 **News**. Keep things topical by tweeting announcements, news and links about your industry or field, and live-tweeting from industry conferences. This all helps position you as an expert.

4 **A daily tip**. Tweeting a daily tip in your area of expertise can be a good way to build a following and keep people coming back for more. I have used @getuptospeed to tweet tips from this book – and to schedule them in advance using HootSuite. Think about what tips, facts or nuggets of information would be useful to your community.

5 **Retweets**. Keep an eye on tweets in your topic area and retweet them. You can keep abreast of these by setting up a 'search' stream in HootSuite or TweetDeck. I have a column set up in HootSuite that displays latest tweets containing the keyword 'publishing'. Whenever I see a link that I think my @publishingtalk followers will find useful, I can retweet it in a couple of clicks. Follow thought leaders, commentators or publications in your industry too, as they can be a good source of retweetable tweets. Add them to a Twitter List so you can easily find them.

6 **An online newspaper**. Use **http://paper.li** to create a daily online newspaper that aggregates relevant blog posts and articles shared by people on Twitter over the last 24 hours. There are various ways you can source the stories, including from everyone you follow, by hashtag, or from people on a Twitter List – such as your 'thought leader' list. I do this for 'The Publishing Talk Daily', which you can find at **http://paper.li/publishingtalk/daily**. This also ensures at least one tweet per day, since the latest paper is announced on your Twitter timeline. You can also set up weekly papers, and have access to more features with a 'Pro' account ($9 per month), including custom branding, email newsletters and your own ads.

Create a Twitter widget

Now that you are promoting your blog on Twitter, promote your Twitter feed on your blog using a Twitter widget. This pulls tweets back onto your blog or website, shows your website visitors that you are on Twitter, and gives a flavour of what content to expect if they follow you – which they can do with a single click.

1 Go to your **Settings** and choose **Widgets** from the left-hand menu.

2 Click the **Create new** button (or the **Edit** button next to a widget you have previously created).

3 Select your timeline source from **User timeline**, **Favorites**, **List** or **Search**. (Normally you will choose **User timeline**.)

4 Select your options – most importantly the **@username** of the account you want to create a widget for. This will usually be your own account, which is filled in by default – but you can use any public Twitter timeline. Other options include width and link colour, but you can leave these at the default settings.

5 Click **Create widget** (or **Save changes** if you edited an existing widget), and copy and paste the code into your site. If you use WordPress, you can create a new **Text** widget in your dashboard (go to **Appearance** and **Widgets**), and simply paste the code there.

Your finished widget will appear in the sidebar of your blog.

Build your followers

Building followers on Twitter is like building up your email list. What's more, the people on the list you're building are all interested in what you have to say – they have *chosen* to follow you. Once you have a sizeable list, you can announce your latest product, service or event – so long as it is genuinely of interest to your followers and you're not doing a hard sell. However, like an email list, you don't want people on there who are not interested in what you're offering. You don't want to randomly broadcast a wasted marketing message – you want to engage your fan base of followers who are actually interested in what you do. You can use 'promoted' tweets to build a following – but you can boost your numbers for free with a bit of effort. The big secret is simply: *follow more people*. At least half will follow you back. But there are a few caveats:

1 **Only follow people who are in your community of interest**. Follow people who are likely to be interested in you and follow you back. Do a keyword search or look at who is tweeting from a conference within your industry by following the hashtag. A more efficient way is to find people like yourself, who are tweeting in your subject area – and follow their followers. Their followers are also likely to be interested in your tweets. To find these people, look at the Twitter directory WeFollow (**http://wefollow.com**).

2 **Stay within the Twitter follow limit**. There is a limit – you can't just follow everyone. Twitter will stop you from following any new people once you hit the limit. However, that limit increases the more followers you have. Anyone can follow 2,000 people. After that, you can follow 10 per cent more people than are following you. So, if you have 5,000 followers, you can follow 5,500 people and no more until you have more followers.

3 **Unfollow people who don't follow you back**. Just like you don't want random, uninterested, disengaged people clogging up your email list, you don't want uninterested people taking up valuable space in your allowance of people you can follow. In this way you can free up space for new people to follow. You can find those people who you follow but who don't follow you by using Friend or Follow (**http://friendorfollow.com**).

This can be a bit time-consuming. But by following this strategy you can incrementally increase your followers to high levels in a relatively short space of time. You may only need to actively increase your followers when you first start using Twitter since, once you reach a critical mass of followers, your Twitter success will build on itself.

Finding followers is easy. Keeping them is harder.

Finding followers is easy. Keeping them is harder. In the same way people can stop subscribing to your email newsletters, they can stop following you on Twitter. If you stay focused on engaging your followers with useful, interesting, regular content, you will not only keep your followers but attract new ones.

Engage your audience

You can engage people on Twitter simply by being useful and creating a topic-based feed of information and links that are valuable to your target audience. But if you want to go further and get people talking about you and your products on Twitter – and therefore making your message visible to their followers – you need to build a bit of buzz, community and conversation.

1 **Be responsive**. Reply when people message you, at least some of the time. Retweet and favourite positive messages. If you get negative feedback, reply to that too where you need to – by DM or email if necessary.

2 **Tweet something sharable**. The most retweeted tweets tend to contain links, photos, videos or quotations. Something interesting, inspiring, entertaining or that solves a problem is more likely to be shared, especially if your followers think it will be useful to their followers.

3 **Host a Q&A**. Invite your community to ask you questions by running a Q&A. This can be a great way to build buzz, especially when you launch a new product. Simply pick a topic, announce your Q&A in advance, and ask people to send you questions via Twitter (by sending @messages to you and/or using a specific hashtag), and answer them. Restrict your Q&A session to a relatively brief period – two to three hours is optimum. During the Q&A, choose the questions you want to answer, retweet them, and then answer them by replying to the questioner, but including a full stop or other character before the @username ('.@username...') so that your reply becomes visible to everyone who follows you, not just those who follow both you and the person asking the question.

4 **Give something away**. Offer a free download in exchange for a tweet. A free service called Pay With a Tweet (**www.paywithatweet. com**) enables you to tap into the viral pass-on potential on Twitter.

Specify the message you want people to tweet, the web address you want to include in the tweet, and a link to your download, and you're good to go. Once someone has tweeted the message (which they can change, but the weblink must be included), they have access to your download. And you have a marketing message visible to their followers.

5 **Run contests**. Engage followers by giving something away. The entry requirement may simply be to follow you, use a specific hashtag or retweet a specific tweet; but you can also run photo contests or pick the first correct or most creative answer to a question. For example, during the London 2012 Olympics, Innocent Drinks launched a creative answer contest called 'tweet for a seat'. Followers could win a pair of tickets to different Olympics events by simply tweeting to @InnocentDrinks who they would take to the Olympics and why. There are tools to help you run Twitter contests, including OneKontest (**http://onekontest.com**). Contests give you an excuse to talk about your products – and get your followers talking about them too.

6 **Offer discounts**. Another approach is to tweet regular time-limited discount codes. For people who are interested in your products or services, it pays to follow you on Twitter since they'll have access to discounts.

7 **Organise a tweet-up**. If you have a loyal following of people who are united by a common interest, consider organising a get-together – easy to do with Twtvite (**http://twtvite.com**).

Manage the workload

So how will you find time for all those updates? Fortunately Twitter plays nicely with most other social networks – so there are plenty of opportunities to aggregate and automate – plus social media dashboards can save you time and help share the workload.

→ **Automate** at least some of your tweets by tweeting your blog with Twitterfeed and setting up a paper.li daily online newspaper.

- → **Aggregate** updates from various other social media services you use, such as your Flickr, Instagram or Audioboo accounts. You can also push status updates from LinkedIn profiles and Facebook pages through to Twitter – but be cautious about this, as your audiences are a bit different. If you want to do it the other way around, this is no longer possible with LinkedIn, but you can make your tweets become updates on your Facebook profile and pages. Do this selectively, though, with Selective Tweet Status (**http://apps.facebook.com/selectivetwitter**) to push only tweets ending in #fb to Facebook.

- → **Schedule** some of your tweets in advance, and release them over time with TweetDeck or HootSuite.

- → **Manage** and monitor multiple Twitter accounts using a social media dashboard such as TweetDeck or HootSuite. Use HootSuite to manage various other social networks too. Use the Pro version to add unlimited accounts, and get your hands on analytics.

- → **Share** the workload. The flipside of managing multiple Twitter accounts is to have several people managing one Twitter account. Assigning 'team members' to your HootSuite Pro account is the best way to do this.

- → **Integrate** Twitter into your daily life by using a smartphone app. The official Twitter app makes it easy to switch between your Twitter accounts if you have several you manage, or you can use TweetDeck or HootSuite apps too. You can also keep HootSuite or TweetDeck open on your desktop computer. Integrate Twitter into your browser experience by using the Bitly 'Bitemarklet'. Sign into your Bitly account, click on **Tools**, then drag the **+bitmark** button to your browser's toolbar.

Measure your results

Finally, has it all been worth it? How do you know if your Twitter strategy is a success? Because there are lots of third-party tools out there to help you, including:

Get Up to Speed with Online Marketing

1 **Count the numbers**. How many followers do you have? You can track the trend over time using TwitterCounter (**www.twittercounter. com**). You can look up anyone's follower stats – not just your own – and show off your own webstats with a TwitterCounter badge on your website.

2 **Track follower locations**. Twocation (**www.twocation.com**) is a useful tool that will show you where your followers are geographically. This is useful for deciding, say, which currency to price your products in, and when to tweet based on time zone. For example, I know that about 55 per cent of my @publishingtalk followers are in the USA – so there's little point in me tweeting before midday in the UK, since half my followers haven't woken up yet.

3 **Analyse your stats**. The amount of traffic that comes to your website from Twitter can be gleaned from your webstats package. If you use HootSuite Pro you will have access to additional analytics.

4 **Click-throughs**. If you use Bitly to shorten your links, you will have plenty of metrics on how many people clicked on them.

5 **Look up your ranking**. Add yourself to WeFollow (**http://wefollow. com**) with up to five topic areas, and see where you sit in relation to the competition according to your 'prominence' score out of 100. This is calculated using an algorithm similar to Google's PageRank – based not just on how established and influential you are, but on the prominence score of your followers.

Twitter best practice

1 **Tweet regularly** to keep people engaged and stay in your followers' timelines. At least once a day, but ideally several times a day. Don't be afraid to tweet the same blog post more than once to increase your chances of it being seen in the timelines of your target readership.

2 **Schedule tweets** using HootSuite – but keep them spaced throughout the day to ensure maximum visibility.

3 **Get the timing right**. When should you tweet? A good time to reach a lot of people is 4 pm – but experiment with your community, and pay attention to the time zone most of them are in. Tweet at weekends too – more people will be more responsive to your messages, yet fewer businesses do this.

4 **Be useful** – tweeting useful links and information is the best way to build a topic-based following. A good rule of thumb here is the 80/20 Rule: at least 80 per cent of your tweets should be useful information, no more than 20 per cent promotions, offers and marketing messages.

5 **Be informal** – keep it professional, but use a conversational, personable tone of voice.

6 **Be sociable** – use hashtags, and retweet and reply to people at least some of the time.

7 **Link to your blog**. As well as tweeting your blog, use the Twitter widget to pull tweets back onto your blog or website.

8 **Include links in your Twitter biography**. Including @usernames in your biog can be useful for linking between accounts so that people can see the person behind a business account, for example. My @publishingtalk biography includes 'Run by @jonreed'. People can click through to my personal account from there if they are interested.

9 **Tweet multimedia**. Enhance your content by including images, video and audio. Upload pictures to Twitter and pictures will also show up in your sidebar. You can include YouTube or Vimeo links in your tweets, and people will be able to play videos on the page and see them in your sidebar. You can also create your own videos using a service such as Telly (**http://telly.com** – formerly TwitVid) or a smartphone app called Vine that enables you to create six-second looping videos. You could use this for quick video demos of products. Tweet audio with Audioboo (**http://audioboo.fm**), such as client testimonials, short interviews at trade shows, or simply to speak directly to your customers.

10 **Promote your Twitter username**. Include your @username anywhere your customers interact with your brand – e.g. on business cards, letterheads, your email signature, product packaging, publications or merchandise.

Take action

→ **Set up** your Twitter account.

→ **Customise** your page with a profile picture, header image and background.

→ **Create** a useful news feed by linking to your blog.

→ **Build** your followers by following people in your community of interest.

→ **Engage** your audience with Q&As, contests, giveaways or tweetups.

→ **Manage** the workload with tools such as HootSuite and TweetDeck.

→ **Measure** your results with tools such as TwitterCounter and HootSuite Pro.

Get on Google+

How to add people to your circle of influence

Chapter Fourteen

Facebook may be the world's biggest social network, with over a billion users. But it is not the biggest website. Knocking Facebook into the number two spot is, of course, the mighty Google. That alone should make Google+ worth a look. But it has some unique features to help promote your business too. Social networking is about building communities, and Google+ offers some innovative ways to do that. This includes its communities feature, video chat with hangouts, and the ability to segment your market and build several discrete communities of interest using circles.

What is Google+?

Launched in 2011, Google+ is the latest social network from Google. If you're sceptical about joining Google's latest attempt to get into the social networking market – well, I understand. There have been previous attempts, often trumpeted as 'Facebook killers' (anyone remember Google Wave?), which sank without trace. Google+ is different. It still exists, it has quickly built up a following, and it has momentum. Google's fourth attempt is its most successful. It has its devotees and evangelists among the social media community, and I think you can have confidence that it will be around for a while.

 You can have confidence that it will be around for a while.

Google+ can look a little confusing at first, but it works in a very similar way to other social networks such as Facebook – it just uses different terminology:

→ Instead of friending or following people, you add them to **circles**.

→ Posts are usually called **stories**.

→ Instead of liking a story, you show your appreciation with a **+1**.

→ As on Facebook, you can **reshare** a story.

The main features on Google+ are displayed down the left-hand side of your page in a vertical navigation bar, though you need to hover over the item shown (initially 'Home') to see the full menu:

→ **Home** – your 'home stream' is equivalent to the news feed in Facebook. It includes latest posts or 'stories' from people in your circles, plus some extra ones. You can filter what you see in your stream by circles once you have some set up – just click the name of the circle you'd like to see stories from. Your right-hand sidebar shows a list of people in your circles who have enabled video chat with you (known as 'hangouts').

→ **Profile** – your profile page is what people will see when they visit your page. The default view is **Posts** – stories that you have posted and shared – but people can also view your **About** page. Other tabs that may or may not be visible to visitors depending on your settings are **Photos**, **YouTube** videos you have uploaded, your **+1s** and **Reviews**.

→ **People** – find people to add to your circles, see who has added you to their circles, and manage your own circles.

→ **Photos** – upload, back up and organise your photos.

→ **What's Hot** – content that is recommended from across Google+, suggested communities, interesting people and pages, plus the latest 10 topics that are 'Trending' on Google+ (similar to trending topics on Twitter, including hashtags).

→ **Communities** – on Google+ communities are a bit like groups on Facebook or LinkedIn. Depending on the settings of the community you want to join, you can either join it instantly and start contributing, or ask to join.

→ **Events** – integrated with Google Calendar, Events are a way of inviting people to and managing events via Google+. Everyone at an event can contribute their photos directly to one shared photo collection. There's even a 'Party Mode' where people can snap and share photos in real time from the event, from their phones.

→ **Hangouts on Air** – a feature that makes Google+ stand out from other social networks is video chat, or 'hangouts'. Start a hangout with up to nine friends, accept hangout invitations from others or chat one-to-one. You can do this from your right-hand sidebar.

Hangouts on Air are hangouts that people have made public. These are also recorded and saved for later viewing.

→ **Pages** – create and manage your business pages from here.

→ **Local** – people can 'check in', review locations and add photos. With Google+ Local, all their reviews and associated photos are visible to everyone on the web, under your name. If you are a local business, such as a coffee shop or a hotel, this is another good reason to add yourself to Google Places for Business (**www.google.com/business/placesforbusiness**).

→ **Settings** – manage your account, security, profile and privacy settings from here.

Why does Google+ work for business?

While, for many people, Facebook is social networking, for many more Google *is* the internet. That alone makes Google+ an important place to be. Everyone who has a Google account, for whichever Google product or service they use, now has a link at the top right of their Google page that notifies them of Google+ updates and allows them to access their profile. Many websites now use the '+1' social sharing button to enable people to post content to their Google+ accounts. It is already embedded in the browsing experience of around half a billion people – and you can reach them by having a presence on Google+.

It is already embedded in the browsing experience of around half a billion people.

In just over six months the platform gained more than 90 million users and now has over 500 million, making it the third largest social network in terms of user numbers. And in 2013 a report by Global Web Index listed it as the number two site (after Facebook) by active usage.

There are useful ways you can engage people on Google+, including with business pages and topic-based communities, as we shall see later in this chapter. But it also works because of the way it changes search and drives traffic.

Search benefits

One of the benefits of having a Google+ account – even if you never use it – is for the search engine benefit. Because Google+ is owned by Google, which page do you think will appear first if someone Googles your name or business name? That's right – your personal profile or business page on Google+! Google+ helps Google to improve its search engine results pages through the information it is able to collect from your social circle. Not only can Google see what you share with your friends, it can see which of your friends are most important to you and how you interact with them. It can promote search results that people from your circles have +1'd, for example.

Traffic benefits

Google+'s '+1' buttons appear in Google's search results and can be embedded in websites. The +1 count that is displayed on each button refers to the number of people who have +1'd that specific web page, and helps people see how popular certain web pages are without visiting them. It pays to use the +1 social bookmarking button: according to HubSpot, websites that use it get 3.5 times more traffic from Google+ than those that don't.

Google+ in action

How a hotel room booking service builds brand awareness with Google+

LateRooms.com is the UK's leading online accommodation specialist, providing discounts of up to 70 per cent off normal hotel room rates on properties in the UK, Europe and the rest of the world. Social media manager Rich Kemp says: 'Our main objective is to raise brand awareness in the social space. Google+ provides us with a unique opportunity as we have a truly global audience, unlike the make-up of our other social channels. Our aim is to create cool content that people want to share with their own social circle and, by doing so, tell the story: the story of who we are, what we do and what we make possible.' Their Google+ strategy includes the following elements:

▶

- → **Segment with 'circles'**. LateRooms ask followers what content they're interested in and puts them into corresponding circles, sharing the most relevant information for that audience.

- → **Post rich content**. Travel content is inherently visual, LateRooms takes advantage of the visual web by posting images on Google+.

- → **Engage face-to-face-to-face with 'hangouts'**. LateRooms.com organised their first hangout with outdoor and adventure expert Ray Mears. Through it, they engaged with all of their fans by offering tips for enjoying an adventurous short break.

- → **Find influencers with 'ripples'**. LateRooms uses Google+'s post metrics called ripples to see how posts spread across Google+. This helps them identify influencers and watch how communities form around specific content.

Get the idea: One of the unique benefits of Google+ is the ability to segment your market with circles and keep your message relevant to your audiences' interests. Use photos and video chat to engage people visually, and look at the metrics of individual posts to measure success and focus your content. Finally, don't be put off by unfamiliar terminology such as circles, hangouts and ripples – all will be explained in this chapter!

Sources: **www.google.com/+/business/case-study/lateroom.html** *and LateRooms*

Get up to speed with Google+

To get started with Google+, the main things you need to do are:

- → Set up your profile.
- → Add people to your circles.
- → Create a business page.
- → Create a community.

Set up your profile

Your personal profile on Google+ is important, as it will help people determine if they think you are worth adding to their circles. First of all, add a header image. Then click **About** on your **Profile** and the **Edit** link below any section you want to update. Two sections that are particularly useful for promoting yourself: **Story** (your biography) and **Links** (including links to other social networks, your blog and business website).

Unlike Facebook there is not currently an option to choose a 'vanity URL' for your Google+ profile – though there are plans to introduce them. Meanwhile, use a service such as **http://gplus.to** or **http://gplusid.com** to create a more memorable URL for your account (rather than a meaningless string of numbers), which you can then promote on business cards, email signatures and elsewhere.

From your profile you can add updates as you would on other networks. These can include photos, videos, events and links. You have a great deal of control over who sees your posts by using a feature unique to Google+ called 'circles'.

Add people to your circles

What are circles?

On Facebook you send friend requests, on LinkedIn you send invitations to connect and on Twitter you follow people. On Google+ you add people to circles. This is a novel approach to adding people to your social network – but a powerful one that solves a problem and helps you market your business.

Are you familiar with that modern dilemma of whether to accept a Facebook friend request from a parent, boss or client? There are ways around this on Facebook. But most people either don't know that you can create lists of friends on Facebook with different permissions levels – or they do, but don't use them because they're not very intuitive. On Twitter it is impossible – you can't even control who follows you and sees your every public tweet.

This is where Google+ has an advantage. You can share posts with who you want to. You can mark updates public, or just share them with specific circles or even individuals. This helps you filter your message to reach the right people – but also keeps your content relevant. I have never been in favour of automatically sharing the same status update across all social networks. But circles aren't just useful for keeping business and personal updates separate: they also mean you can segment your market. Use them to target only the people who are most likely to be interested in a blog post, product or special offer.

However, just because you have added someone to your circles doesn't mean they will necessarily see anything you post; that will only happen if someone adds *you* to their circles. It's an asymmetric system – like Twitter. When you add someone, their public posts appear in your home stream and the streams of any circles you have added them to. The posts they share with specific circles are only visible to you if you are in one of those circles. And the reverse is true: if someone adds you, they will then see your public posts. They will *also* see any content you post to any circles you have that they are in. This is how segmentation works in Google+.

So, you need more people to add you to their circles in order for Google+ to become a useful marketing tool. Like Twitter, the way to do this is through following (adding) more people, and sharing useful content.

Create your circles

You can create new circles whenever you add someone, which you can do from their Google+ page. There are essentially two ways to categorise people into circles: by relationship and by interest:

→ **Relationship circles** might include 'Family', 'Friends' and 'Clients' – use these to manage your professional relationships, and to keep your personal and business lives separate if you wish.

→ **Interest circles** might include 'Publishing', 'Social Media' or 'Baking' – use these to segment your marketing messages to the most receptive audience and keep your content relevant.

You can create as many circles as you want and call them what you like.

You can create as many circles as you want and call them what you like – experiment and see what works for you. You might have different circles for family, friends and colleagues, and you would add new connections to whichever circle you see fit. You can also add people to multiple circles.

But you can take this a step further. While people will receive a notification that they have been 'added to circles' by you, they won't know how many, which ones, or what they are called. No one else sees your circles. This gives you freedom to call them anything you like – including, for example, 'Prospects' or 'Competitors'. Avoid anything offensive though, just in case! Think of circles as a mixture of inbound and outbound messages: some may be more useful for market research or keeping abreast of your industry, and some may be more important for reaching out to your community. Here are some suggestions.

Inbound circles

→ **Thought leaders** – who are the key bloggers, speakers or commentators in your industry? Add them to a circle to help you keep your knowledge current.

→ **Suppliers** – add current and potential new suppliers to a circle to keep up with any new services they offer and as a handy place to turn when you're looking for a new web designer, graphic designer, shop fitter, etc.

→ **Competitors** – who is your competition? Keep an eye on what they're up to, and what new products and initiatives they are launching.

→ **Locals** – do you run a local business such as a bar or restaurant? Add people who live locally to a circle called 'Local' or named after your town or city. This will help you keep up with local news and target locals with details of events or offers.

Outbound circles

→ **Prospects** – who have you had enquiries from but not actually signed up as a client yet? Who have you met at a conference or trade fair who could benefit from your services? Keep these contacts warm by posting content that reminds them what you do.

→ **Clients** – who are you working with at the moment, or who have you worked with in the past? You might have several circles for different types of client so you can target specific offers to each.

→ **Interest circles** – create several interest circles based on different interest groups your business serves.

Start sharing

Once you have your circles set up, you can share posts or 'stories' with people in them. You can make your posts visible to:

→ **Public** – anyone on the internet, including those searching Google, so it's a good idea to make most of your posts public.

→ **Your circles** – anyone who is in at least one of your circles.

→ **Extended circles** – your circles plus people in their circles.

→ **A community** – if you choose to share with a community, you can *only* share with that community and not 'Public' or 'circles' as well. See the later section on communities for details.

You can also tag other people in your circles on your Google+ posts, as you can in Twitter with an @username or Facebook by typing @ and then a friend's name. Type + followed by someone's name, and choose the correct person. This becomes a link to that person's profile, and they will receive a notification that they have been tagged, unless they have opted out of notifications.

Circles are an important concept to understand, as they are central to how Google+ works – and, used well, are a powerful marketing tool. But they are also dynamic, so edit and re-organise your circles as often as you like, and to keep your messages relevant to the right people.

Quick win

Find more people to add with shared circles

Circles are by default private – no one knows which circle you have added them to or what it's called. But there is an option to share your circles – just click the blue 'Share' button on a circle you are viewing to make it public. This can be posted in your public timeline, or shared with specific circles or people. People you share your circles with in this way can then add the people in your shared circle (or a selection of them) to their own circles, or create a new circle based on yours. However, even then, people won't see what you have called your circle. The flipside to this is that you can use circles that other people have shared to speed up the process of

---

finding and following people within your community of interest. A couple of ways to find these are:

1 **Search Google+** for **'shared a circle with you'**. Although the circles that people share don't come labelled with a name, the person sharing the circle will often give you a clue in their status update – e.g. 'Enjoy this circle of photographers from around the world!'. Include a keyword term in your search to look for circles shared in a particular topic.

2 #CircleSunday is the Google+ equivalent of Twitter's #followfriday. Search this hashtag for recommendations of people to follow – which can include individuals, but tends to be shared circles.

In addition, check out Recommended Users (**www.recommendedusers. com**) for a directory of people on Google+ listed by topic area.

Create a business page

Businesses can create pages, develop a following and build relationships in much the same way as profiles. Profiles have an 'Add' button and pages have a 'Follow' button, but both work in the same way. Individuals can add people and pages to their circles; and pages can also organise followers into circles. This may mean you choose to use a business page to develop business connections and segment your market, and reserve your profile for personal relationships and interests. But be aware that more people will add *people* to their circles than businesses – and a page can't even add someone to its circle until they have first added or mentioned that page.

Other differences to bear in mind include:

→ Pages can't mention you unless you're connected to them.

→ Pages have the +1 button but can't +1 other pages, nor can they +1 stuff on the web. (But like profiles, they can +1 inside Google+.)

→ Pages don't have the option to share to 'Extended circles'.

→ Local pages have special fields that help people find the physical location of the business.

To get started:

1 **Create your page** – visit **http://plus.google.com/pages**, click **Create a Page**, and choose the options most suited to your business.

2 **Customise your page** – the profile basics include your tagline and a profile image, which can be your logo.

3 **Promote your page** – Google+ will now prompt you to promote your page. Wait until you have customized your page further and started sharing some updates.

4 **Optimise your page** – follow Google+'s prompts to create an effective page.

Set up Google+ Direct Connect

With the launch of Google+ Business pages, Google also rolled out a new integration between Google+ and Google search called Direct Connect. People who want to find a company's Google+ page can now simply add a '+' in front of the company name in a Google search to go directly to that company's Google+ page. However, in order to get this working for your business, you need to verify your page:

1 Go to your Google+ page and click **connect your website** under the **Get Started** section.

2 Choose the option to display a button on your site to encourage visitors to become subscribers to your Google+ page.

3 Add the code to your website – and you are eligible to be included in Google Direct Connect. This doesn't happen automatically, though. Just like when you launch a new website it takes a little while for the Google algorithms to pick it up and include it in search results, Google also uses an algorithm to determine which companies get included. Promoting your Google+ page on your website and elsewhere can help get your business listed.

Frequently asked questions

What are Google+ hangouts?

Google+ hangouts are essentially video chatrooms. All you need to get started is a computer and a webcam. You can start a hangout with up to nine friends, accept hangout invitations from others or chat one-to-one. You might consider hangouts for video meetings with a project team (and create a circle for your team members), for customer support, focus groups, or for tutorials with small groups. Although you can only have nine people in your hangout, you can also go live from your laptop and stream it publicly if you check **Enable hangouts on Air** before you start. What's more, you can record your hangout, which gives you some video content, for your website, your YouTube channel, your YouTube tab on Google+, and to share on other networks. You don't need any special software for this – every Hangout On Air is automatically saved to your YouTube account. You could use these for regular Q&As or tutorials that you announce in advance to your community.

Create a community

Pages are useful for building a following around your company or products. Communities help build brand loyalty, and position you as an expert in a particular field. They are most effective if they focus on discussion around topics related to your business. Communities on Google+ are the equivalent to groups on Facebook or LinkedIn, and are a powerful way to reach a lot of people at once. There are two main ways to use them: join other communities, and start your own.

Communities help build brand loyalty.

Join some communities

Go to the communities tab to see suggestions and any communities you are already a member of, and to search for communities to join in your topic area. Communities may be public or private – i.e. joined instantly by anyone, or subject to approval of requests to join. Join some that are relevant to your interests and/or business. I am a member of a number of writing and publishing communities, for example, including Digital Publishing, Writer's Discussion Group and amwriting. I find the discussions and links shared useful – and there are also occasions where I can contribute usefully, sometimes sharing what I'm doing or a blog post.

1 **Be selective**. Don't just join as many communities as you can. Join those relevant to your topic area where you have something useful to contribute – and don't just dump links to your blog.

2 **Post to the most appropriate category**. Communities come with categories built in – a bit like discrete forums within the community. You can view all the posts shared in a community, or view them by category. This helps keep discussions focused and relevant.

3 **Observe the guidelines**. Communities often have guidelines attached. It pays to follow these so you don't annoy other members – or get kicked out. Some strictly forbid any self-promotion, while others encourage it – so long as you post to the right category.

4 **Post from your home stream**. You can share posts with communities from your home stream/profile too, without even visiting the community you wish to post to. However, you can only post to one community at a time this way, and you cannot post to public/people/circles at the same time.

Start your own community

Once you have familiarised yourself with how communities work by joining a few, it is time to create your own. If you start your own community, you can begin building your own list of members and don't have to worry about breaking someone else's community guidelines. To get started, just go to your communities tab and click the **Create community** button.

1 **Keep it open**. I would generally recommend making communities public to make them more visible and attract greater numbers. If you choose to make your community private, people can still see it if you want them to – or you can hide it from searches.

2 **Add your 'About' text**. Tell us who the community is for, who is behind it, and include a link to your website for more information.

Get Up to Speed with Online Marketing

3 **Set guidelines**. Look at the guidelines for some of the communities you are a member of, and adapt those that chime with how you want your community to behave.

4 **Moderate posts** to maintain their value. You can also add more moderators to your community. Moderators can add and edit categories, remove posts or members and add additional moderators.

5 **Use categories** to organise discussions.

6 **Invite people to join** your community – but only when you have some content to give them a flavour of what to expect. Promote your community on your Google+ profile page, company page, on your blog and via your other social media channels.

Manage the workload

There is not currently a way to set up automatic posting of updates or blog posts to Google+ – but there are ways to monitor, update and manage your activity efficiently:

1 **Add your pages to HootSuite** – Google+ is another service you can add to your HootSuite dashboard, though you can only add pages. Use HootSuite to post to your Google+ page at the same time as you post to other networks, and to manage multiple Google+ pages.

2 **Access from your Mac** – if you use a Mac, 'Tab for Google+' is a free Mac app that allows you to monitor and access Google+ direct from your menu bar.

3 **Update from anywhere** – if you use a smartphone, the Google+ app is great for updates and notifications on the move.

4 **Share the workload** of maintaining your Google+ community by adding additional moderators from within your community: click **members** below your community's photo; click the drop-down menu to the right of the member you'd like to add as a moderator; then click **Promote** from member to moderator. Share the workload of managing pages by appointing additional administrators to your pages or additional team members to your HootSuite Pro account.

Measure your results

Clearly Google+ has the ability to be integrated more deeply into Google Analytics than any of its competitors – but whichever webstats service you use, you can look at how much traffic is coming from **plus.google.com** – and which links to your own website you have shared there are most popular. You can also use your HootSuite Analytics (if you have a Pro account) to measure click-throughs.

For some deeper insights, use a third-party service called CircleCount (**www.circlecount.com**). This provides a wealth of information about your Google+ account, including which of your posts were most popular, and which days of the week and hours of the day result in the most engagement, which can help you decide when to post and focus your content.

For analytics on individual posts, there is a great built-in service called Google+ ripples. This creates an interactive graphic of the public shares of any public post on Google+, showing you how a post has rippled through the network and helping you discover new and interesting people to follow. Ripples shows you:

→ who has publicly shared the post and the comments they have made;

→ how a post was shared over time;

→ statistics about how a post was shared.

You can access ripples from any public post in your stream. Just click the drop-down arrow at the top of the post that you're curious about and click **View Ripples**. Be aware that this doesn't necessarily display all the data on a post: only data for the previous 53 days is shown, and only public reshares will be shown.

Google+ best practice

→ **Share photos**. Share images and infographics to increase the viral spread of your content.

→ **Add recommended links**. Use the **Links** section on your profile and your page (both under your **About** tab). Add links to your website and blogs – but also to one or two of your best blog posts or to lead-generating offers. You could also link to your email signup form. Think about links that will help drive traffic and sales – and share these with your circles too.

→ **+1 content** from within Google+ on your page, and from other websites on your profile.

→ **Encourage sharing**. Use the +1 button on your website and under every blog post you write. You can include this alongside other social bookmarking buttons using a WordPress plugin.

→ **Segment** your market using circles, using a mix of relationship and interest circles, and use them for inbound and outbound communication.

→ **Search for shared circles** to find more people to add to circles and increase the number of people who have you in circles.

→ **Create a page** to promote your brand on Google+ and set up **Google+ Direct Connect** to make it easier for people to find your page via Google.

→ **Promote your page**. Once you've gone to the trouble of creating a Google+ page, let people know about it. Promote it in your email signature, and especially on your blog and website.

→ **Join communities** and share content with them – you can do this from your home stream. Make sure you follow the community guidelines and post to an appropriate category.

→ **Start your own community** to promote brand loyalty and position you as an expert in your field.

Take action

→ **Create** your Google+ profile.
→ **Add** people to your circles and think about how you can segment your market.
→ **Create** a Google+ page for your business.
→ **Join** Google+ communities – and create your own.

Pique interest with Pinterest

How to use the visual web to attract attention

Chapter Fifteen

We've seen throughout this book how the visual web is influencing online marketing and how images have become a key ingredient of social media, from the success of Instagram to the prominence given to images on social networks. No wonder, then, that one of the biggest social media sensations in recent years is a social network based entirely on images: Pinterest. According a report by Experian, by 2012 – within two years of launch – Pinterest was already the third most popular social network after Facebook and Twitter (though in terms of web traffic rather than user numbers). It was the fastest site ever to break through the 10 million unique US visitors mark according to comScore, and had over 70 million users by July 2013. Pinterest may have crept up on us – yet the statistics show that pinning is winning.

The statistics show that pinning is winning.

What is Pinterest?

Pinterest is a virtual corkboard – a place to 'pin' your interests. You can create and arrange boards on specific topics and pin images to them. These images can be uploaded, but are usually pinned from websites using a 'Pin It' button on your browser toolbar, and link back to them. You can add descriptions, and other people can like and comment on your pins, and 'repin' (share) them on their own boards. Just like on Twitter, you can follow people on Pinterest and they can follow you. But you can be a bit more selective about it: you can either follow all of someone's boards, or just those boards that interest you the most.

The main navigation options are in a bar across the top of your page:

→ **Pinterest** – the Pinterest logo in the centre of the bar is also your link to your 'Home Feed' default view. This shows the latest pins from everyone you follow, plus your latest notifications of anyone who has commented, liked or repinned one of your pins.

→ **Browse** – clicking on the square icon with three horizontal lines at the left of the screen opens a list of about three dozen categories from architecture to tattoos. Useful for browsing pins by category.

→ **Search** – enter a keyword into the search box, and them filter your results by Boards, Pins or Pinners. Useful for finding boards to follow, pins to repin and pinners to follow.

Click the + button to create a board or manually upload an image and specify which web address you want it to link to. For example, I do this with images of individual pages of *Publishing Talk Magazine* and link them all back to the sales page for the issue the article comes from. You can also add a pin from a website here, though normally you will use the 'Pin It' button for this.

Click your account name on the right-hand side to reveal the following drop-down options:

→ **Your Boards** – this links to your profile, which is what other people see when they visit your Pinterest URL, e.g. **pinterest.com/ publishingtalk**. You can also see a couple of things casual visitors can't: 1) a 'Create a board' button at the top and 2) up to three 'Secret boards' at the bottom.

→ **Your Pins** – your latest pins displayed in reverse chronological order, regardless of which board they were pinned to.

→ **Your Likes** – the latest pins you have liked.

→ **Settings** – modify your email notifications here, and link to your Facebook and Twitter accounts – useful for reaching a wider audience with your pins.

There is also a **Help Center**, an invitation to **Find Friends** and a link to **Log Out**. Finally, click the speech bubble icon next to your name to see your latest notification.

Why does Pinterest work for business?

If Twitter is good for sharing links, and Instagram and Flickr are good for sharing images, Pinterest offers the best of both worlds. With Pinterest you can share images that encourage click-throughs to your website, blog and other websites. This is the point of Pinterest from a marketing point of view: it's really just another social bookmarking site, since people use it to share links to other websites. But because you are sharing an image from the web page you are linking to, rather than providing a text link to it, it has a much higher click-through rate than text-based social bookmarking sites such as Digg or Delicious. According to a 2012 Shareaholic study it drives more referral traffic than Google+, YouTube and LinkedIn combined. The links are also more permanent than those shared on Twitter, as they are more likely to be discovered, shared and clicked on long after links shared on Twitter have disappeared way down your timeline.

Each image you pin links back to its source – and some of these should, of course, link to your own website. You can also upload images, and specify where they should link to. This is what drives the referral traffic from Pinterest. Use automatic tweets and Facebook shares of your pins and the effect is multiplied.

You can benefit from Pinterest without even having an account by making your own web pages pinnable. For this you need to do two things:

1 **Include images**. Include at least one image on every web page or blog post you want people to be able to pin. Make sure this is a reasonable-sized one too, not just a thumbnail. If you don't have images, people can't pin your page.

2 **Encourage sharing**. Use a 'Pin It' social bookmarking button – either the button provided by Pinterest or a WordPress plugin such as Shareaholic, which includes a 'Pin this' button.

If you sell physical goods, Pinterest seems an obvious place to promote your wares with attractive pictures of your products that people will want to share. These pins will all link back to the product page on your website, and you can even add prices to your descriptions and they will appear as flashes across the corners of your pins. However, don't just pin stuff you're selling – the culture of Pinterest is more like a glossy lifestyle magazine than a product catalogue.

 These pins will all link back to the product page on your website.

Pinterest in action

How a jewellery designer drives sales with Pinterest

Beth Quinn (**www.bethquinndesigns.com**) is a self-taught jewellery and mixed media artist living in Arizona. She has around 3,000 followers of her Pinterest boards at **pinterest.com/bethquinn**. Filled with boards that display things she loves, from vintage décor to Paris to Marie Antoinette, her profile helps communicate her aesthetic style and brand personality. Just one of her 35 boards, 'Her Handmade Jewelry', directly promotes her products with images pinned from her website.

Beth began by using Pinterest to create mood boards and to post ideas and images of her jewellery. Towards the end of 2011 another Pinner spotted one of her charm necklaces bearing the words 'with brave wings she flies' (**pinterest.com/pin/97953360614840293**) and repinned the image. Two days later she had received 20 orders for the necklace, and over the next two months 300 more. Two years on, Beth still sells around 30 of these necklaces per month due to Pinterest. Subsequently another necklace got more than 1,500 pins and 400 likes, causing traffic to spike to 70,000.

Beth says: 'More and more people comment all the time that they have found me on Pinterest, and it really is a driving force behind my business. I still get a high volume of hits from people pinning my jewelry. Since it is free advertising, I can't say enough good things about using Pinterest as a venue to promote yourself!' Spending three to five hours a week on Pinterest, Beth typically sees 10,000–15,000 hits per day. As well as driving sales, her Pinterest activity has led to more retailer enquiries and magazine features.

Get the idea: Don't use Pinterest purely as a product catalogue – think about ways you can communicate your brand personality with attractive images. Sell a lifestyle rather than a product, and don't be afraid to mix up business and personal boards. Beth says: 'It is important to use Pinterest to create a style that makes your business brand and creates a statement.' Make sure images of your products are attractive and shareable too: Beth puts time and effort into styling and photographing every piece herself. Encourage people to pin images from your website on their own boards by adding the 'Pin It' button to every product page.

Sources: **www.boston.com/business/specials/small_business_blog/2012/02/pinterest_isnt_for_every_small_business.html, http://blog.intuit.com/marketing/how-pinterest-drives-one-jewelry-designers-sales/** *and Beth Quinn*

Get up to speed with Pinterest

You can set up a personal and/or business account on Pinterest – and then start pinning images to your boards. We will look at the best ways to do this to promote your business in the following steps:

→ Create your Pinterest account(s).

→ Create some boards and start pinning.

→ Promote Pinterest on your website.

Create your Pinterest account

First of all you need an account. You can now choose either a personal or business account.

→ Go to **http://pinterest.com** and click the red **Join Pinterest** button; or, if you want to set up a business account, go to **http://business.pinterest.com** and click the **Join as a Business** button.

→ Sign in with Facebook, Twitter or create an account using your email address.

→ Pinterest will invite you to click on a few topics so it can suggest people to follow. You need to choose at least one category, and will end up following a few people – but you can unfollow them later if you want.

→ Upload a profile photo, add a web address and include a short biography.

→ If you chose to set up a business account, you will have a couple of extra fields to fill in: a **Contact Name** (the person managing your account – this can be anyone and is not publicly shown) and a **Business Type** to be selected from a drop-down menu of eight options including Professional, Brand, Media and retailer – plus 'Other'. This can be changed later.

→ On your Settings page (**http://pinterest.com/settings**) you can also choose whether or not to push your pins through to your Facebook profile and/or Twitter. You can also choose to post individual pins to Twitter/Facebook manually if you prefer.

If you already have a personal account, you can convert it to a business one. All you need to do is go to **http://business.pinterest.com** and click the **Join as a Business** button as above – but *while logged in to your personal account*. You can go straight to **https://pinterest.com/business/convert**. You can also update any other information from your personal profile, such as your biography. Be aware that Pinterest has a new set of terms of service (TOS) specifically for business accounts using Pinterest for marketing, which you will be asked to agree to.

Business accounts on Pinterest look just like personal ones. So why bother? Well, since Pinterest now provides resources specifically for businesses, and may roll out new ones in future, it makes sense to identify yourself as a business if that is primarily how you intend to use it. Keep an eye on latest developments for businesses at **http://business.pinterest.com**. You could also choose to create separate personal and business accounts. But whether you have a personal account, a business account, or both, is really a matter of personal preference. It will also depend on the type of business you run, and how closely it is tied to you as a person.

Add the 'Pin It' button to your toolbar

Before you start pinning, you need to add the 'Pin It' button to your browser's toolbar. You can upload images to Pinterest and enter the website you want them to link to manually. But Pinterest works best – and saves you time – when you use the 'Pin It' button.

1 Go to the **Goodies** page at **http://about.pinterest.com/goodies**.

2 Scroll down until you see the red **Pin It** button – and drag it into your browser's toolbar.

Quick win

Verify your website

If you join as a business, you will be asked to go through an extra step of verifying your website. You can also do this with a personal account. This is worth doing, as it will allow you to highlight your full web address on your profile and adds a checkmark next to it here and in search results.

▶

→ Click your name in the profile menu to go to your profile.

→ Click the pencil icon on your profile.

→ Make sure you have added your website to the **Website** field.

→ Click **Verify Website**.

→ Click **Download Verification File**. It should look something like: pinterest-xxxxxx.html.

→ Upload this to your website – making sure it is on the root domain, for example **www.publishingtalk.eu/pinterest-xxxxxx.html**. You can delete this after your website has been verified if you want.

Create some boards and start pinning

Now you can pin an image from any website onto one of your boards, simply by clicking the Pin It button in your toolbar. Your pins can be organised by theme or topic into 'boards'. You should add descriptions to your boards – and to your pins. Pinterest suggests five default boards:

1 Products I Love

2 Favorite Places & Spaces

3 Books Worth Reading

4 My Style

5 For the Home

These can be deleted or renamed if you wish. So long as you're logged in, you will see an 'Edit' button beneath each board, which enables you to change the name of your board, add a description and category, and invite others to pin to your board. You will also see a 'Change Cover' button when you hover over a board. This enables you to choose a different cover for your board from the pins it contains.

You can also create 'Secret boards'. These are only visible to you and people you invite to them. You can make any new board you create secret by editing its settings – and you can change a secret board to public later, maybe once it is populated with some pins and you're ready to show it to the world. But you can't switch it back again and make an existing public board secret.

You can include links in your descriptions, including:

→ **Web addresses** – normally you will rely on the image you pin to click through to the website it came from, but this can be useful if you want to include another web address.

→ **Hashtags** – these will become clickable links to everyone's pins that include that hashtag.

→ **@mentions** – for example, if I post an image of the contents page of a magazine, I will add a description such as: 'What we're talking about in issue 4 of *@Publishing Talk* Magazine'. This becomes a link to the Publishing Talk Pinterest profile and means that wherever this is repinned and seen by someone new, not only can they click through to the web page from the image pinned, they can click on the username and visit the Publishing Talk Pinterest account.

Ten things to pin

Once you've got the hang of boards and pinning, it's time to get strategic. How will you use your boards and what will you pin to engage your audience and drive traffic to your website?

1 **Your products**. Listing your products is still the most obvious marketing method. But do this sparingly, or keep a separate board for products and pin other images related to your brand too.

2 **Your own images**. Pin your own web pages to your Pinterest boards, so people can repin them on their own boards, and you can build up the number of pins that link to your site.

3 **Your blog posts**. Pin every post to Pinterest – making sure each has a pinnable image, of course. If a post doesn't seem to fit, create a new board so it does. Take advantage of the referral traffic Pinterest drives to benefit your blog.

4 **Contests**. Photo contests are popular on many social networks, and Pinterest is an obvious place for these. Invite people to submit photo entries by pinning them to their own boards with a specific hashtag in the description (so you can track entries). Repin entries

to one of your own boards set up for the contest, and judge the winner, perhaps partly by number of likes or repins. You can also use third-party services to manage contests. Use Piqora (**www. piqora.com**) to configure, launch, manage and analyse various types of promotions, including sweepstakes, contests, coupons and instant wins.

5 **Promotions**. Use boards for specific, themed promotions. These might be seasonal or tied to a topical event.

6 **Locations**. The default 'Places and Spaces' board is popular on Pinterest, and images of locations are widely repinned. Do you work in or visit clients in photogenic, pinnable places? This isn't confined to high-end tourism – even if you work in an office, showing us your workplace, who works there and what they're doing can be an engaging way to give followers a 'backstage pass' to your business.

7 **Lifestyle**. Think about lifestyle images at one remove from what you actually do or sell. For example, UK online real estate portal Rightmove (**www.rightmove.co.uk**) pins images of inspiring properties and interiors, with separate boards for 'Bedrooms', 'Living Rooms', 'Kitchens', etc. as well as locations, celebrity homes and DIY tips at **pinterest.com/rightmoveuk**.

8 **Tutorials**. Use Pinterest to share practical tips and information related to your business, particularly where you can do this in a visual way, such as with before-and-after photos (e.g. a furniture restoration project), the finished product (e.g. a recipe for lentil soup), or to show a technical skill (e.g. car maintenance). Link each of these pins to a blog post where people can find more information. Because you can also pin videos, pin any video tutorials you create too.

9 **Infographics**. For more abstract information, infographics are very popular on Pinterest, and you'll find plenty of them in your field of interest that you can repin. I have a board for 'Social Media Infographics', for example. Hopefully people will find these useful and interesting – and some will discover my 'My Books' board that way too. Even better would be to create your own infographics. You might need to conduct some original research and commission a graphic designer to do this – but you will then benefit from repins and click-throughs to your own website.

Get Up to Speed with Online Marketing

10 **Text**. Although images work best, it is also possible to pin text. Use **Share as Image** (**http://shareasimage.com**), which lets you highlight text anywhere on the web and turn it into an image. This is most useful for pinning inspirational quotations, which people tend to like and repin.

Frequently asked questions

Doesn't Pinterest breach copyright in images?

In the early days of Pinterest copyright was a big controversy, with many people objecting to their images being pinned to other people's boards. With a few exceptions (e.g. professional photographers and image libraries), I didn't get it. An image pinned doesn't seem much different to an image displayed in Google image search results. They both just link to the source – and you *want* to encourage links to your website, don't you? For anyone who really wants to prevent pinning there is now a snippet of opt-out code that they can put on their websites. But the real danger with Pinterest is *not* having images on your website. When I first set up my personal Pinterest account (**pinterest.com/jonreed71**) there were many web pages that I wanted to link to – but couldn't, simply because there were no images on the page. No image, no link.

Promote Pinterest on your website

If you have a 'cloud' of social media icons on your website, make sure Pinterest is one of them so that people can see that you're on Pinterest and follow you there. In addition, Pinterest offers buttons to encourage pinners and followers and widgets to display pins and boards on your site. These tools allow people to see your activity, and encourage people to follow you. Get started at **http://about.pinterest.com/goodies**.

The most important of these is the Pin It button you will find under **Pinterest Widgets**. This is a social bookmarking button you can add to your website rather than the 'Pin It' bookmarklet you previously added to your browser toolbar.

If you use a WordPress blog, I suggest you don't actually bother with the Pinterest 'Pin It' button, but instead use a WordPress plugin such as Shareaholic to add a row of social bookmarking buttons underneath every blog post and/or page. Just make sure that, when you configure the plugin in your back-end, Pinterest is one of the buttons that appears.

Manage the workload

There are two services that will allow you to schedule pins to keep your followers engaged throughout the day – though both charge a monthly fee, so are better suited to bigger brands or heavy users of Pinterest:

→ **Pingraphy** (**www.pingraphy.com**) enables you to upload pins in bulk as well as schedule them. You can't schedule repins or upload original pins to schedule, but you can pin and schedule images you find online. Log in using your Pinterest account and then use their toolbar button instead of Pinterest's when you want to pin something. You'll be able to see your most recent pins and quickly see if you have likes, comments or repins. Currently $12 per month for a basic subscription or $28 per month for a premium subscription.

→ **Curalate** (**www.curalate.com**) offers more advanced scheduling. Instead of just choosing the board and date/time to post your pins, you can edit the URL and all of the details from your dashboard. Currently $99 per month for up to four users.

Measure your results

There are various free third-party tools to help you find out if Pinterest is working for you, including:

→ **PinReach** (**www.pinreach.com**) tracks your repins and likes and to find out which pins and boards are the most popular – and which result in click-throughs to your site.

→ **PinAlerts** (**www.pinalerts.com**) sends an email alert whenever someone pins something from your website.

→ **Piquora** (**www.piqora.com**) offers comprehensive analytics and will help you identify your top-performing content on Pinterest and track your most engaged and influential pinners, and the popularity and reach of your own boards and pins. You can also use it to get analytics on your competitors, so you may end up knowing more about their Pinterest performance than they do themselves!

The two paid for tools that you can use for scheduling also offer analytics:

→ **Pingraphy** (**www.pingraphy.com**) helps you track repins, likes, clicks and reach for every pin, and identify your top performing boards and most influential followers.

→ **Curalate** (**www.curalate.com**) offers 'analytics for the visual web', covering both Instagram and Pinterest. It will find pins from Tweets and Facebook 'likes' originating from Pinterest so you can see which other social networks are driving traffic. It also offers monitoring and listening tools, and custom promotions.

Plus in March 2013 Pinterest rolled out its own free metrics tool: Pinterest web Analytics (**http://business.pinterest.com/analytics**). This allows you to track the number of people pinning from your website and the number of pins – plus repinners and repins of the initial pins. You can also track referral traffic, as both clicks and unique visitors to your site. To get started:

1 Make sure you have a verified website. If you have a website listed on your profile with a check mark next to it, you're verified. (If not, follow the steps set out on pp.237–8.)

2 Once your website is verified, go to the top-right menu and click on Analytics.

3 Select time frames to analyse, see where pins are being posted, and more.

Pinterest best practice

1 **Make your pages pinnable**. Include images on any pages you want people to pin, and make sure they are large enough to pin and attractive enough to encourage clicks.

2 **Promote a lifestyle**. Use Pinterest to showcase your brand personality in a fun way, rather than just promoting products or services directly. Glossy magazine-style aspirational lifestyle images are popular on Pinterest, from homes and gardens to food and travel. What lifestyle does your brand promise?

3 **Share information**. Infographics and tutorials get a lot of shares on Pinterest, particularly for more service-orientated businesses. Use it to create a resource and show your expertise.

4 **Promote your products**. Promote products and services by pinning images from your blog sparingly. When you do, add prices where appropriate so that they are displayed in the corner of your pin.

5 **Link your pins** to your own web pages. You can upload images as well as pin them from your website.

6 **Promote your blog posts**. Pin every post to one of your boards. Pinterest has become a major driver of traffic for many bloggers.

7 **Go viral**. Automatically tweet your pins and share them on Facebook to amplify the viral nature of Pinterest.

8 **Create contests** and promotions, and use Piqora to help you manage them.

9 **Like and repin** images posted by other pinners, and follow other people's boards.

10 **Use hashtags** to tap into something topical or trending, and use @mentions to link to other Pinterest accounts in descriptions or comments.

Take action

→ **Set up** a personal and/or business Pinterest account.

→ **Add** the 'Pin It' button to your browser toolbar.

→ **Create** some boards and pin shareable images to them.

→ **Promote** Pinterest on your blog or website.

Get help

Part Five

Achieve more by outsourcing

How to find someone to help you achieve your vision

Chapter Sixteen

Can you do all this yourself? Or should you hire someone? There is a lot you can do on your own to promote your business online, cheaply, easily and effectively. Indeed, it is better to do many things yourself, such as writing blog posts and status updates, to retain your own authentic, personal voice. And if you follow the advice in the 'Manage the workload' sections of this book, you are less likely to be overwhelmed by the responsibility.

However, it doesn't hurt to call in a bit of help when you need it – either to help you plan your marketing, do the technical media production tasks, administer your accounts and updates, or simply to save time that you could better spend doing what you do best – running your business. As management guru Peter Drucker says: 'Do what you do best, and outsource the rest.'

It doesn't hurt to call in a bit of help when you need it.

In most cases you won't be recruiting full-time staff – you'll be hiring freelancers for a one-off project or for a small amount of regular extra help. There are a number of scenarios when you might want to hire someone to help with your online marketing, including:

1 You understand how to use most social media tools – but you need some market intelligence or research to help you decide which to focus on and how best to use them to reach the right people.

2 You have some great creative ideas for content – but lack the technical skills to set up a blog, design a bespoke Facebook page or edit a video.

3 You're an experienced web designer/blogger/video producer, etc. – but you're spending too much time on media production when you should be focusing on your business.

4 Your blog/podcast, etc., has come to a standstill because you no longer have the time or interest to do it all yourself.

5 You are busy developing new products and don't have the time to maintain your social media as you once did.

6 You or your team are overwhelmed by the additional workload and responsibility of maintaining your online marketing.

Get Up to Speed with Online Marketing

The type of help you hire will depend on the size of your organisation, what skills gaps you or your team have, and the sort of tasks you need doing.

Audit your tasks

The first stage is to identify what needs doing and where the gaps are. Draw up a task list, and decide which things can be done in-house and which you want to outsource. Which tasks do you, realistically, have the time to do alongside your other responsibilities? Which tasks are critical to be done in-house to maintain your unique personal voice and brand? Where does your expertise lie, and which tasks would be better outsourced to a specialist?

> # The first stage is to identify what needs doing and where the gaps are.

You can do this at the level of your entire marketing plan, or for a specific project or campaign. Tasks can then be broken down into smaller chunks than 'produce a podcast'. You might, for example, want to record interviews, but then hand over the raw files to an audio producer who can edit them, add some music and output them as discrete MP3 files – and then take it back in-house to upload to your blog yourself.

Think about the roles that relate to each task (whether in-house or outsourced), and who will own each one. Draw up a grid a little like this:

Role	Task	Owner
Strategy	Draw up an online marketing plan for new product launch	
Graphic design	Design a podcover Create a web design concept for a new blog Design email newsletter template	

▶

Role	Task	Owner
Editorial	Write blog posts Subedit blog posts from contributors Conduct interviews for podcast	
Web design/ development	Create bespoke WordPress theme for blog Create ecommerce site Create bespoke Facebook page	
Production	Editing, post-production and output of video clips	
Admin	Set up accounts on Twitter, Facebook, LinkedIn Set up Twitterfeed for blog Sort out email newsletter databases	
Monitoring	Collate webstat reports and metrics from Facebook, YouTube, etc.	

Tasks you might outsource

Some of the more common tasks you may consider outsourcing include the following:

Web design

Web design is something generally not best attempted yourself – unless you have a good grounding in HTML, CSS and PHP. If you don't speak code, you can still get a professional-looking website up and running quickly using WordPress. You might still want a web designer to hack into the code and customise the look, feel and functions of your site though, to make it bespoke to your business.

Search Engine Optimisation

Do you need a SEO specialist? Or can you focus on generating regular, good blog content, maybe a few ads, and let Google do the rest? SEO consultants can help you reach a bigger market – and save you money on Google Ads. Some web designers will include this in their service too. If you're starting out, I would suggest seeing what results you get from your own efforts first.

Ghost-writing

Is it authentic to hire someone to ghost-write your blog? It's a tricky one. While this may work for some people, I would be cautious about handing over my online reputation to someone else. However, so long as you see and edit these posts before you publish them, and ideally put them in your own voice, it's no less authentic than a newspaper editor commissioning an editorial. You will, after all, have briefed on the topic – the research and writing just happens to have been done by a freelancer. You're still providing valuable content to your readership, in the niche topic area you have identified. And it's better than blogging yourself to death or neglecting your blog for months because you're too busy.

Social network updates

No time for all those tweets and Facebook status updates? Can you get someone else to do it? Perhaps. It depends what your updates are. This is unlikely to work so well for personal updates and replies that are (not really) from you. But it might work for a more topic-based feed of links to blog posts and articles that you think your fans and followers will find useful. You might also involve other people in your team – perhaps stating in your Twitter biography who tweets are from, and signing each one with the initials of the person tweeting, to maintain a level of personal connection. If you have a lot of content to tweet – such as a database of tips – you might want some help pre-scheduling a load of tweets to publish over a period of time. Use HootSuite for pre-scheduling – and upgrade to HootSuite Pro to enable several people to log in and send/ schedule tweets. And don't forget that, if you want to tweet blog posts, you can set up an automated feed for that using Twitterfeed.

Facebook pages

Since Facebook made its pages more customisable there has been a proliferation of services that will create bespoke tabs for you, or enable you to do it yourself through a drag-and-drop interface. These can work well, especially if you're not at all techy – but they tend to be expensive. In particular, watch out for those that charge a high monthly subscription fee, as you could end up shelling out a lot of money in the long term – and your carefully crafted pages will disappear if you stop paying. On balance, I think it's better to pay a developer a one-off fee for something that works for you long term. Or learn how to create and update basic pages yourself.

Where to find help

The best advice I can give you is to use Elance (**www.elance.com**) rather than searching for outsourcing companies based in specific countries. This is a global online marketplace that matches up freelancers and outsourcers for just about any job you can think of. Simply post the job you want doing, and sit back and wait for the bids to come in from all over the world. Some bids will be from individuals, and some will be specialist outsourcing or VA companies with whom you may subsequently develop an ongoing business relationship. Pick the one you want to work with, and pay their fee in advance via your PayPal account. It is held 'in escrow' until the job is completed to your satisfaction. A rating and reviews system maintains the quality of suppliers, and provides useful reviews of jobs completed.

The vast array of tasks you can outsource this way includes:

→ Web design
→ Blog development, maintenance and writing
→ SEM/SEO
→ Banner ads
→ Graphic design
→ Email newsletter maintenance and writing
→ Audio editing and transcription
→ Market research
→ Business plans
→ Marketing plans

→ Recruitment

→ Virtual assistant/administrative tasks

... and many more. See a list of the top 100 jobs you can Elance at **www.elance.com/p/100-projects-outsource.html**.

When to hire a consultant

While you might want to kick-start your marketing by having someone draw up a marketing plan for you, in many cases it is not necessary to hire a consultant for individual campaigns unless you are a big business. It is better to brush up on the principles and practices, and familiarise yourself with those online marketing tools that seem most suited to your business. After all, you are the one who will be tweeting or blogging much of the time.

The boom in social media has been followed by a boom in social media consultants – a term that sometimes feels as derisory as 'snake oil salesman'. Some consultants do great work for their clients. Some are more hype than help. And there is a wide range of services on offer. How do you cut through the hyperbole and inflated claims and decide who is genuinely worth your investment? Who will help grow your business? And what can they help you with?

Who will help grow your business?

Here are some questions you should ask before hiring a consultant:

→ What projects have you worked on previously for which clients?

→ What benefits did you bring to them?

→ What metrics would you use to measure results?

→ Do you have your own blog/Facebook page/Twitter feed, etc.? How successful is it?

→ Do you offer help with marketing strategy, media creation and/or maintaining a social media presence?

→ What specific tasks can you help with?

When to hire a social media manager

This is one for the larger companies – or something to bear in mind for the future when your small business grows! Many organisations started off by experimenting with social media in a fairly uncoordinated way – fine at first, as most of this stuff is free, and it can be a good way to find out what works for you. But, at some point, it can become hard to maintain all the blogs and updates, and a proliferation of accounts may spring up, duplicating effort and sending out a confused brand message. You need to restrain people from going off and doing their own thing (while not squashing their enthusiasm). You need to restore order and manage your social media.

If you work for a large organisation and have reached that critical mass of social media activity that becomes hard to track and control, it may be time to consider hiring a social media manager. This is someone who can work across an organisation, coordinate roles and responsibilities, help draw up strategies and marketing plans, and assist with the actual work of maintaining blogs, podcasts, video and social media sites. He or she may also hire in technical or production help where needed. When hiring a social media manager, look within your organisation first. Who is most enthusiastic in your department? Who really gets it? You may have some home-grown talent ready and willing to take on a new role.

Alternatively, you may opt for a committee-based solution: appoint a committee of existing staff whose role it is to draw up a corporate level social media marketing plan, with clear aims and objectives; and then draw up some guidelines and policies. These should state how various tools – such as Twitter – are used by the organisation, and who is responsible for what. Include also any naming conventions to be used if there are many Twitter or Facebook accounts to be used across the organisation.

When to hire a virtual assistant

If you are a start-up or entrepreneur, you are unlikely to have the luxury of a social media manager. It will probably all be down to you. That's not a bad thing, as social media often works best for small businesses, and small businesses often communicate best when the owner's personality comes across. However, before you despair of the enormous workload involved, bear in mind that you can hire in help quite cheaply in the form of a virtual assistant (VA). He or she can be a great asset to your small business. Not just for marketing, but for all sorts of tasks.

In his bestselling book *The 4-Hour Workweek*, Tim Ferriss advocates outsourcing as a means of leveraging your time and resources via 'geoarbitrage'. That means 'exploiting global pricing and currency differences for profit or lifestyle purposes' – or charging your clients in pounds or dollars and paying your suppliers pesos or rupees. Examples he cites of outsourcing companies you can use to achieve this include Brickwork India (**www.brickworkindia.com**), based in Bangalore, India's 'Silicone Valley', which specialises in Remote Executive Assistants who can perform a wide variety of tasks on a time zone to suit you.

The outsourcing revolution has moved on a little since then: we've had a banking collapse, and outsourcing isn't quite as cheap as it once was. India and the Philippines are still good value, and there are talented technical experts to be found who speak excellent English. But Brazil and Bulgaria are also on the rise, and it is easier than ever to find VAs all over the world for a reasonable price, including in the USA, which some people prefer for geographical reasons.

A VA can take on a wide range of tasks remotely, from maintaining blogs to doing market research to audio editing to helping with email newsletters. There are plenty of tasks and functions where it makes more sense to get someone else to do, in order to save you time and have them done with more expertise than you possess.

It can be alarming at first handing over control to someone at a remote location – especially when you hand over logins and passwords – but you will soon reap the benefits of not doing it all yourself. It pays to draw up very detailed instructions, even process flowcharts, for specific tasks that need doing. Some people use Camtasia (the screen capture software mentioned in Chapter 8) to record online tasks such as blog maintenance. It can be a very quick way of communicating, on screen, exactly what you need doing.

When to hire a technical expert

You can also hire in technical experts for specialist functions such as video production, graphic design and web design. Your VA can probably help you outsource these tasks too, if they are beyond his/her skillset. For example, I don't claim to be a graphic designer – I always outsource these tasks to freelancers who are far more talented than me. *Publishing Talk Magazine* is beautifully designed, for example – but not by me. I can design websites, but I rarely do these days – I outsource web design to save my time for things that it is better spent on, such as developing my business, creating courses and writing.

Media production is a specialist skill you might not want to tackle yourself. It is also a very time-consuming one. Every minute of finished video you watch could have taken up to an hour to edit. Although the equipment and software is cheaper than ever, making it more accessible than it used to be, you still need a certain level of skill and flair to produce something that looks professional enough to put in front of your customers and prospects. Yes, a certain hand-made charm can be OK, especially if your customers are more interested in the content you're sharing than your production values; but you may end up saving some money and a lot of time, *and* come away with a better piece of media, if you call in a professional.

How to manage your outsourced projects

Sometimes outsourcing is a simple matter of finding the right person with the technical expertise you need for your project, and then working closely with them until it is delivered. Sometimes it is an ongoing relationship, such as with a VA. Sometimes, for large projects involving several people, some more sophisticated project management is required.

I'm based in London yet have outsourced tasks to people based overseas. I also regularly use freelancers based in the UK, many of whom I almost never meet in person. I keep in touch by email, sometimes via Skype – and I manage large projects that involve several freelancers, such as web developers, graphic designers and copy writers, using an online collaborative project management tool called Basecamp (**http://basecamphq.com**). I use Basecamp all the time – to manage client projects and to deliver resources to my workshop participants. I even used it with my publisher to project manage the writing of this book!

If you want to collaborate on documents, spreadsheets and presentations in real time with your team or with freelancers, Google Drive (**http://drive.google.com**) is free and incredibly useful. Dropbox (**http://dropbox.com**) is also useful for moving large files around and sharing them with collaborators, as well as simply for accessing your files from anywhere with an internet connection.

Finally, why not use social media as a management tool? You can use various social media tools to work with freelancers on a project, or a virtual team of people you regularly work with. Instead of Skype, why not have a meeting with your virtual team using a Google+ hangout? If it makes sense to have discussions on a Facebook group or blog, remember that you can set these to private. You can also use 'secret' Pinterest boards and nominate several pinners to a single board – useful for creating virtual mood boards for a new product or brand. Or you could do this publicly and invite comments!

Why not use social media as a management tool?

However you source, assemble and manage your team, and whether for discrete projects or ongoing business functions, there are online tools to help you find help with your online marketing. But don't let go of everything. Remember that the reason your online marketing works, particularly your social media marketing, is *you*: your authentic voice, personality and passion. That's probably part of the reason you started your own business in the first place: to do things in your own unique way, follow your own interests and pursue a passion. Never be afraid to be yourself online. You may be surprised how much business this generates – even unintentionally. Resist the urge to be a bland corporate clone, or to hand your social media presence over to someone else. You can't outsource you.

Outsource the parts of your marketing, and your business, that you either can't do, don't want to do, or don't have the time to do.

Then focus on what you enjoy, what you do best, and where you can add the greatest value to your business. And have fun with it: you've worked hard to build your business – now see it grow with online marketing!

Take action

→ **Audit** your tasks and decide what help you need.

→ **Find** help via Elance.

→ **Manage** your projects with Basecamp.

→ **Manage** your team via social media.

→ **Do what you do best** – and outsource the rest!

An A–Z of online marketing

Aggregation – the process of gathering together content from websites, blogs, or other forms of social media, often using RSS feeds.

Archive – on blogs, archives are collections of older posts usually organised by month. You may still be able to comment on archived items, unless the blogger has closed comments for older items.

Article marketing – sites such as Ezine (**www.ezine.com**) enable you to write articles for distribution to a wide audience, with your biography, byline and web address. Well-written articles increase your credibility and attract new leads, but they can also boost your search engine rankings due to incoming links from these high-ranking sites.

Authenticity – the sense that something or someone is 'real'. If you can show personality and passion in social media you will build more trust than a bland corporate voice.

Autoresponder – in email marketing, autoresponders are automatic emails that are sent when someone subscribes to your mailing list. These emails may be a one-off welcome message or link to a free download; a series of emails over a specific time period, such as daily tips for a week following subscription; or an up-selling message a specific interval after a sale is made.

Blog – a website with dated items of content (or 'posts') in reverse chronological order. Posts are usually organised into categories, may also be tagged with keywords, and should allow comments. Blog posts can include images, video and audio as well as text. Blogs can usually be subscribed to using an RSS feed and are great for driving traffic to a site and boosting search engine rankings. Blogs are easy to set up using tools such as Blogger, Typepad and WordPress.

Blogroll – a list of favourite blogs displayed in the sidebar of your own blog showing which blogs you read regularly and/or other blogs that your readers may be interested in.

Call to action – a clear message contained on a website or piece of social media such as a blog post, podcast or video, to encourage people to do something specific as a result of engaging with your online media. Once you've got someone on to your website, or to listen to your podcast, etc., what do you want them to do? Sign up to your newsletter, download a white paper, visit your blog?

Circles – a way of organising and categorising people you follow (or 'add to circles') on Google+.

Categories – a pre-specified way to organise content, or a taxonomy – for example, a list of categories in the sidebar of a blog that allows readers to browse the blog by subject.

Comments – blogs may allow readers to add comments under posts, and may also provide a feed for comments as well as for posts.

Communities – online communities are groups of people communicating mainly through the internet. They may be members of a community website, or members of a group on a generic social network (such as a LinkedIn group or Google+ community). Blog-based communities also exist as communities of people who are regular readers of a blog.

Content may refer to text, images, video, audio, or any other material that is on the Internet.

Content management system (CMS) – a piece of software that allows you to add to, edit and update content on your site with no need for technical knowledge of HTML code. WordPress can be used as a CMS.

Conversation through blogging, commenting or contributing to forums is the currency of social networking.

Conversational index – a measure of the impact of a blog, calculated as the number of comments divided by the number of posts, either for a whole blog, a blog category or a time period. Aim for a number greater than 1.

Creative Commons (http://creativecommons.org) – an alternative to copyright that facilitates the sharing of content online by attaching a Creative Commons licence specifying, for example, that content may be reused with attribution.

Cross-browser compatibility – test your website to make sure it works in all major browsers, including Internet Explorer, Firefox, Safari, Google Chrome and Opera.

Crowdsourcing refers to harnessing the skills and enthusiasm of those outside your business who are prepared to volunteer their time contributing content and solving problems.

Dashboard – the 'back-end' control centre of (e.g.) your blog, from where you can manage posts, comments, pages, blogroll, categories, plugins and your blog's appearance via themes and widgets. Can also refer to your dashboard on your webstats or email marketing service etc.

Events – real-life events can be organised on social networks, for example Facebook events can be created by individuals, groups or pages. Google+ also has an events function, and Twtvite can be used to organise events via Twitter. Great for promoting launches, seminars and other events where you have a following on these networks.

Feed – see RSS.

Forums are discussion areas on websites, where people can post messages or comment on existing messages.

Friends, on social networking sites such as Facebook and MySpace, are contacts whose profile you link to in your profile. On some sites people have to accept your friend request before you are connected. On Twitter they are called followers and on LinkedIn they are called contacts.

Groups – on social networks, groups are pages that can be set up by anyone with a profile and invite others to join. They usually give members the ability to contribute content and discussions. Available in Facebook, LinkedIn, and Google+ (where they are called communities).

Hangouts – video chat service on Google+ that can be shared with up to nine people and optionally live streamed in public and saved to your YouTube channel.

Hashtags – are used not only in Twitter but also Pinterest, Instagram, Facebook and Google+ to group updates or posts together by subject. They are keywords prefixed with the # symbol and become links that can be clicked on to view a timeline of recent updates or posts that include the hashtag.

Information architecture is a term used to describe the way content is organised on a website, usually displayed as a flowchart of key pages.

Measurement – measurement includes tools such as webstats and third-party services such as TwitterCounter. Most social networks have their own analytics built in, and HootSuite Pro users have access to HootSuite Analytics across a range of networks.

Newsreader – a website or desktop tool that acts as an aggregator, gathering content from blogs and similar sites using RSS feeds so you can read the content in one place, instead of having to visit different sites.

Pay per click (PPC) – any form of online advertising where you pay a small amount each time someone clicks on your ad, including Google AdWords and Facebook Social Ads.

Pages – on Facebook, pages are now the default way that businesses and brands promote themselves. Many use bespoke pages or 'tabs', which can be created with an iFrames app. Business pages are also available for LinkedIn and Google+ users.

Permalink – the web address (URL) of a specific blog post – its 'permanent link'. The blog post title usually links to the permalink.

Photo sharing – uploading, organising and sharing your digital images to e.g. Instagram or Flickr.

Pingback – lets you know if someone links to one of your blog posts and automatically notifies you, so you can see what people are writing about you.

Podcast – audio or video files than can be subscribed to using RSS and automatically downloaded whenever a new episode is published.

Post – a post is an item of content on a blog. Usually text, but can also be images, video or audio.

Profiles – the information that you provide about yourself when signing up for a social networking site. As well as a picture and basic information, this may include your personal and business details, a biography, and your web address.

Retweet – a retweet is a Twitter status update that is quoted or passed on. Either use the syntax: 'RT @getuptospeed:' followed by the text you are quoting; or click the retweet link which becomes visible when you hover over a tweet.

Ripples – a tool for measuring the impact of a post on Google+. Shows an interactive graphic of the public shares of any public post on Google+ and how a post has rippled through the network.

RSS – an acronym for 'Really Simple Syndication'. This allows you to subscribe to content on blogs and other social media and have it delivered to you through a feed. Blogs you subscribe to may be displayed in an aggregator website like Google Reader directly on your desktop using software called a newsreader. Podcasts are usually managed through a service such as iTunes.

Search – people search for information on the internet using a search engine, of which Google is the most widely used. But they also search Facebook, Twitter, YouTube, iTunes etc., so it is important to have a presence on these sites too.

Search engine marketing (SEM) – a form of online marketing that promotes websites by increasing their visibility in search engines such as Google or Bing. You can improve your position on search engine results pages (SERPs) through a combination of search engine optimisation (SEO), paid-for placements (i.e. Google AdWords) and boosting incoming links (e.g. through article marketing).

Search engine optimisation (SEO) – the process of improving the volume or quality of traffic to a website from 'natural' search results as opposed to paid-for placements on SERPs. This involves editing the content and HTML code of a website to increase its relevance to specific keywords and to remove barriers to the indexing activities of search engines.

SERP – Search Engine Results Page.

Social bookmarking – saving the address of a website or item of content on a social bookmarking site like Delicious. If you add tags, others can search your bookmarks too.

Social currency – you need to use social media to be able to use it for marketing purposes. By being present in the social media space (e.g. having a Facebook profile, a blog, a Twitter account), you build 'social currency'. This gives you 'permission' to use the medium to communicate your marketing message – so long as it is relevant and useful to the people you are communicating with.

Social media may be thought of as the collection of tools people use to publish, converse and share content online, including blogs, podcasts, video and social networks. Social media marketing is an approach to marketing based on building relationships with people online. It may be thought of as permission-based marketing or conversational marketing.

Social networking sites are places where users can create a profile for themselves, and socialise with their network of friends and contacts using a range of tools such as adding friends, posting messages, links and other content, importing blogs, and creating groups, pages and events. The most popular include Facebook, Twitter, Pinterest, Google+ and LinkedIn.

Subscribing – the online equivalent of signing up for a magazine: you get new content delivered as it is published. Relates to blogs via RSS feeds, but also podcasts (via e.g. iTunes), YouTube channels, Twitter feeds, email lists, etc.

Tags – keywords attached to a blog post, bookmark, photo or other item of content so you and others can find them easily through searches and aggregation. Tags can usually be freely chosen – and so form part of a folksonomy – while categories are predetermined and are part of a taxonomy.

Tag cloud – a widget you can add to your blog to show the most commonly used tags. The more often a tag is used, the larger the font size. Your readers can see at a glance what you write about, and click on the tags displayed, making it another way to navigate to your blog's content. Can also be used with categories.

Trackbacks – provided by some blogs as a facility for other bloggers to leave an automatic comment. They are usually indicated as a specific URL, often the permalink for a particular blog post. By using this URL as the link for someone else's blog post that you link to on your own blog, an extract of your linking text automatically appears as a comment on the original blog post.

URL – stands for 'unique resource locator', and is the technical term for a web address e.g. **http://www.getuptospeed.biz**.

URL shorteners such as **http://bitly.com, http://tinyurl.com** and **http://snipurl.com** enable you to make the most of your 140 characters in a tweet by reducing the length of URLs you want to link to. Bitly also provides metrics to show you how many people have clicked through on your links.

Unique URL or **unique landing page** – a web address that is only ever mentioned in one place, such as a podcast, video or another website (including e.g. Flickr or Twitter). The URL then automatically refers on to the page you want people to land on, such as a product page, a signup page for an email newsletter, etc. This enables you to track exactly how many people who took action landed on your ordering page as a result of watching a video, listening to a podcast or visiting a website.

Usability testing – you should test how easy it is to use your site with a variety of experienced and non-experienced users within your target market. Do this by observing them complete a specific task – such as using a contact form or locating a specific product or piece of content – and take notes. Make changes to your site if testing throws up issues that need addressing.

User-generated content (UGC) – any text, photos or other content that is contributed to a site by its users. Examples are Wikipedia, Digg and Flickr.

Video has taken off since the wide uptake of broadband. Sites such as YouTube and Vimeo make it easy to upload and share videos. These sites also provide code for each video to enable you to embed the video in a blog post or website. It's usually best to keep them short – no more than three minutes, provide useful content that people will value, and provide a URL for people to click through to.

Virtual worlds – online places like Second Life (**http://secondlife.com**) where you can create a representation of yourself (an avatar) and socialise with other residents. In some ways these are just another social network – it is usually possible to join groups and add people to your friends list – but one with a rich graphical interface that has to be learned first, creating a higher barrier to entry than, say, Facebook.

Web 2.0 – a term coined by O'Reilly Media in 2004 to describe a second generation of web services including blogs, wikis, social networking sites and other internet-based services that emphasise collaboration, sharing, participation and self-publishing rather than less interactive, static websites (Web 1.0). What we used to call Web 2.0 is now more commonly referred to as social media.

White paper – a free downloadable document, usually a report or guide, used to educate people and help them make decisions. Often used to generate sales leads, establish thought leadership, make a business case, or to educate customers. Can be used as an incentive to sign up to your email list.

Widgets are stand-alone mini-applications you can embed in websites or a desktop. These may help you to do things like subscribe to a feed, pull in content from another site, display comments from your Twitter followers, etc.

Wiki – a web page or website that can be edited collaboratively. The best known example is Wikipedia (**http://wikipedia.org**), an encyclopaedia created by thousands of contributors across the world. Depending on their permissions level, people can add and/or edit pages. Create your own wiki using **www.wikispaces.com**.

Wireframe – a simple diagram showing the layout of key elements of a web page.

Wisdom of crowds – the idea that individual contributions to a website – such as items of content, rankings and ratings – produce robust, reliable results that are greater than the sum of their parts. For example, Wikipedia is more reliable and authoritative than often thought, since inaccurate or insufficiently referenced information will soon be challenged or edited by others.

Index